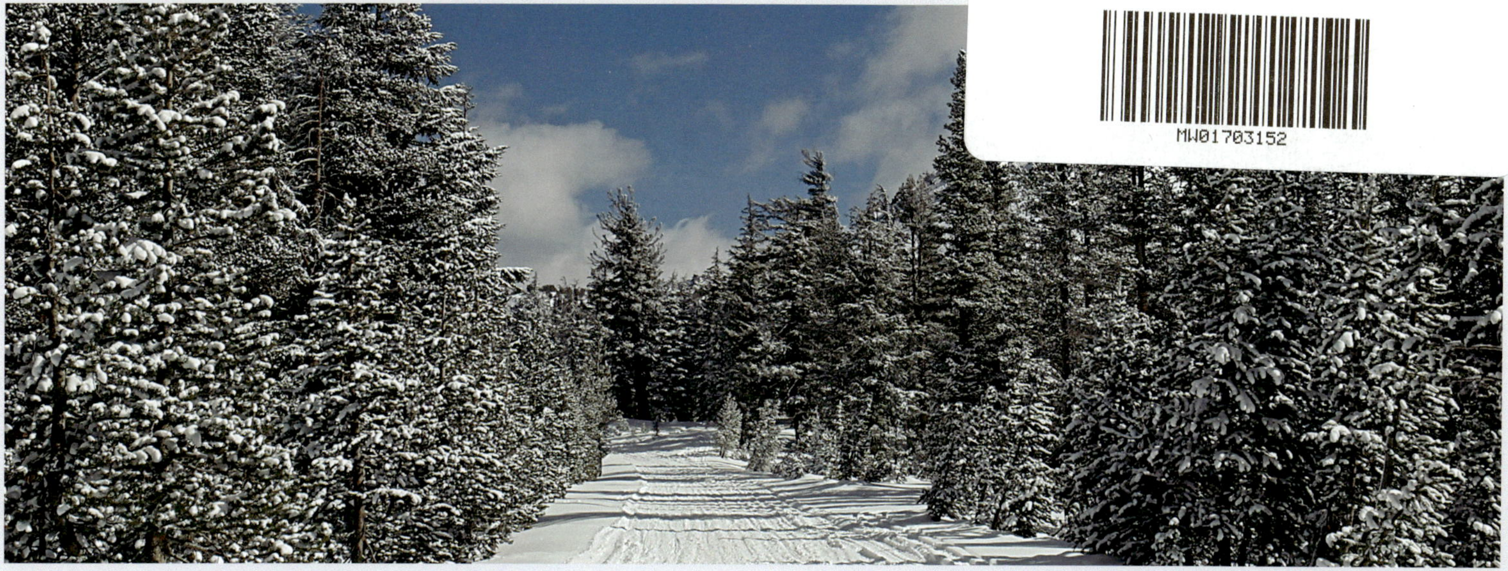

For You

by Maggie Lynch

Contents

Align for Magic

Create a gateway to float
Into the unconscious
Make a causeway that allows for magic
To come through

We know
An inner world exists
We just don't know its depth
Do not fear what you can so easily visit

Love the unknown
Live with uncertainty
See in darkness
Be with depth

Then you can talk with the stars
Aligning the gateways
Of all your consciousnesses

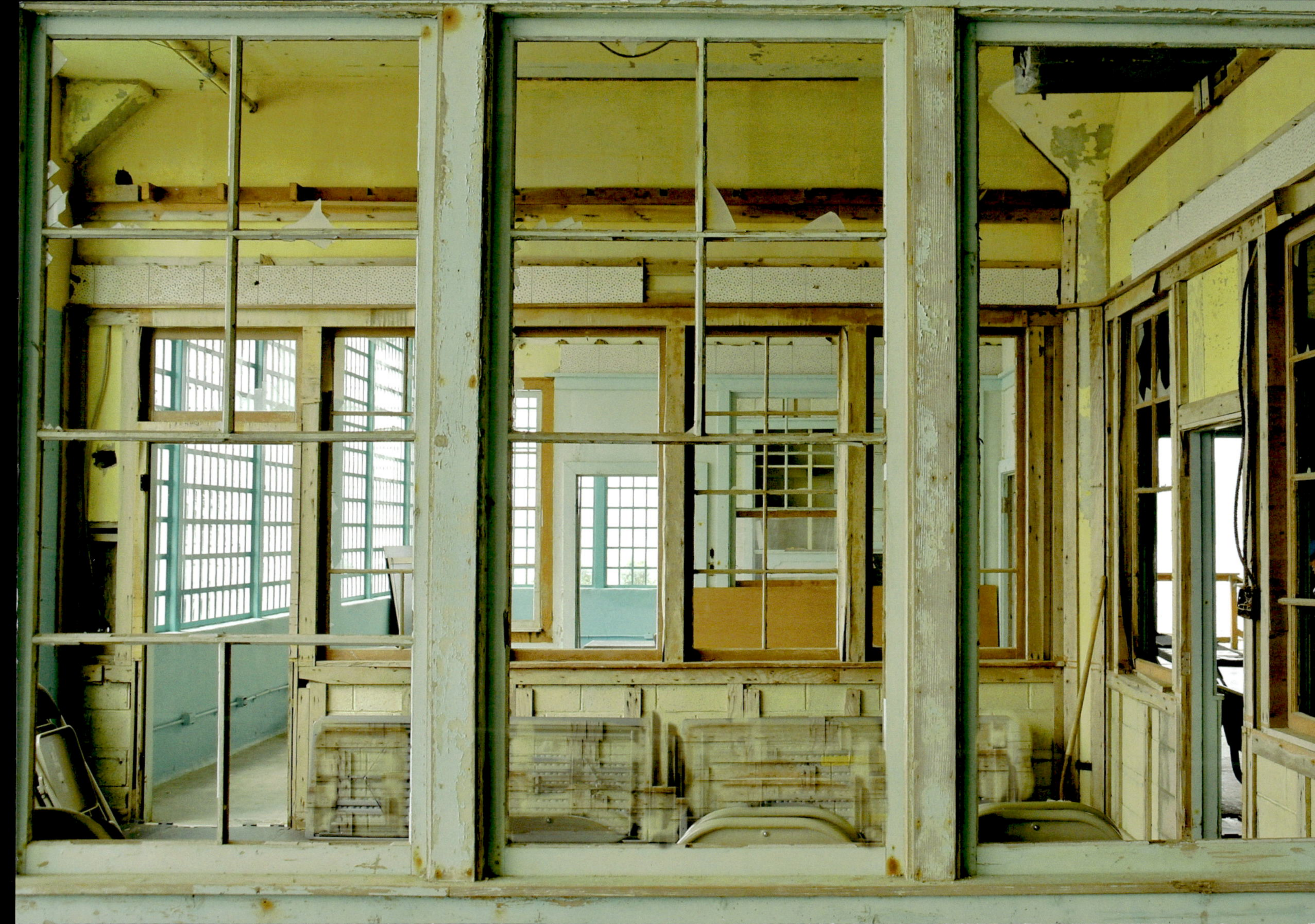

Beauty If You Let It

Beauty is a beacon
It will lead you to gratitude
If you let it

Gratitude is a wave
It will fill your heart
If you let it

It will enter the back and the front
Fill every cell
If you let it

The awareness of time
With the contemplation of beauty
Is as exciting as any mystery

Beauty is a power
You can feel it
If you let it

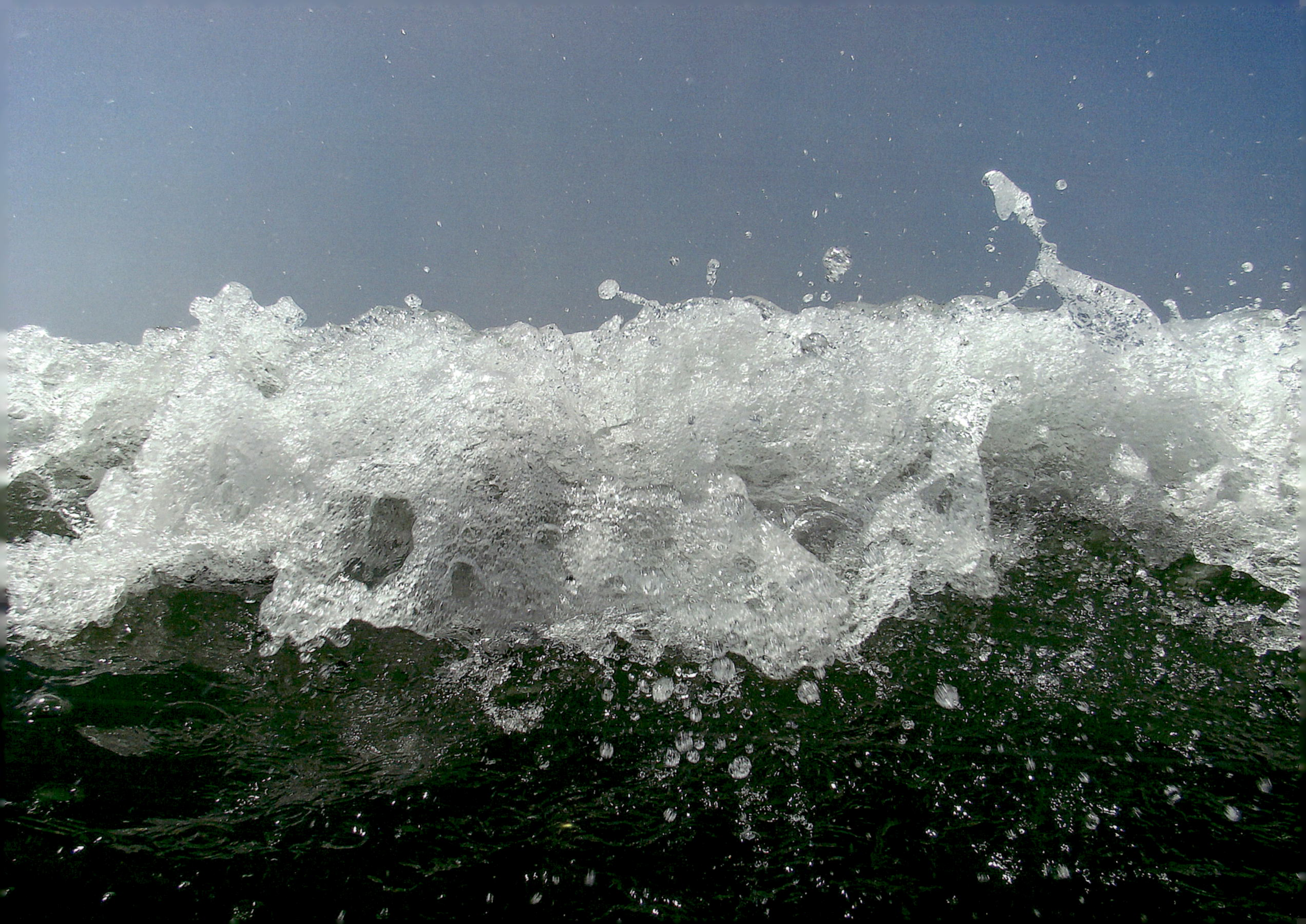

Energy Around You

Even when you don't trust yourself
You can feel a oneness
With the beautiful unknown

Thinking about energy around you
You have that energy around you
Gently invite the mystical
The mysterious and the magical

Is the mystical gentle?
Is the mysterious gentle?
Is the unknown gentle?

As you think it, so it must be
Gently build the trust
To feel your oneness

All the easier to reach
The beautiful unknown
As nothing can resist the gentle.

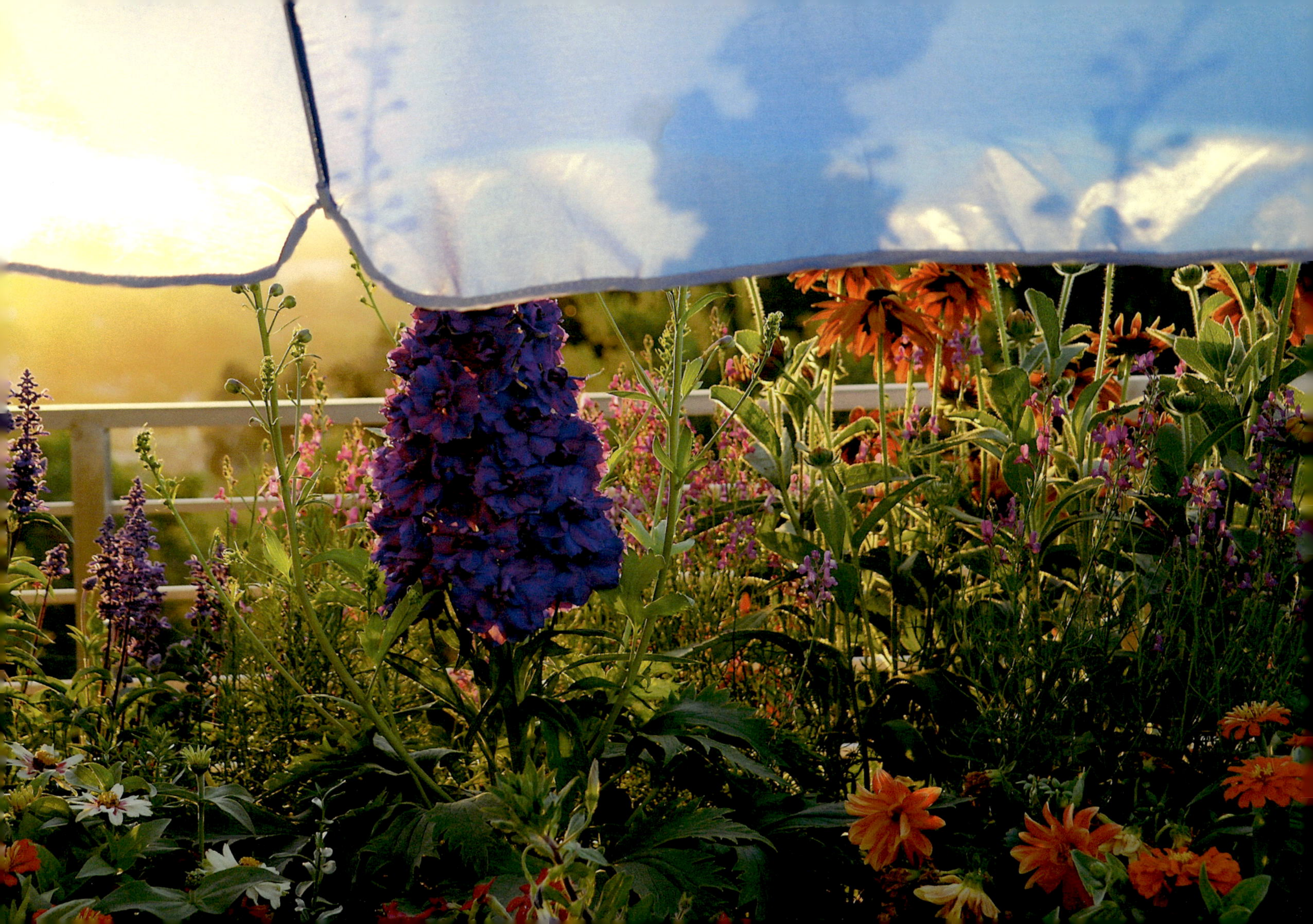

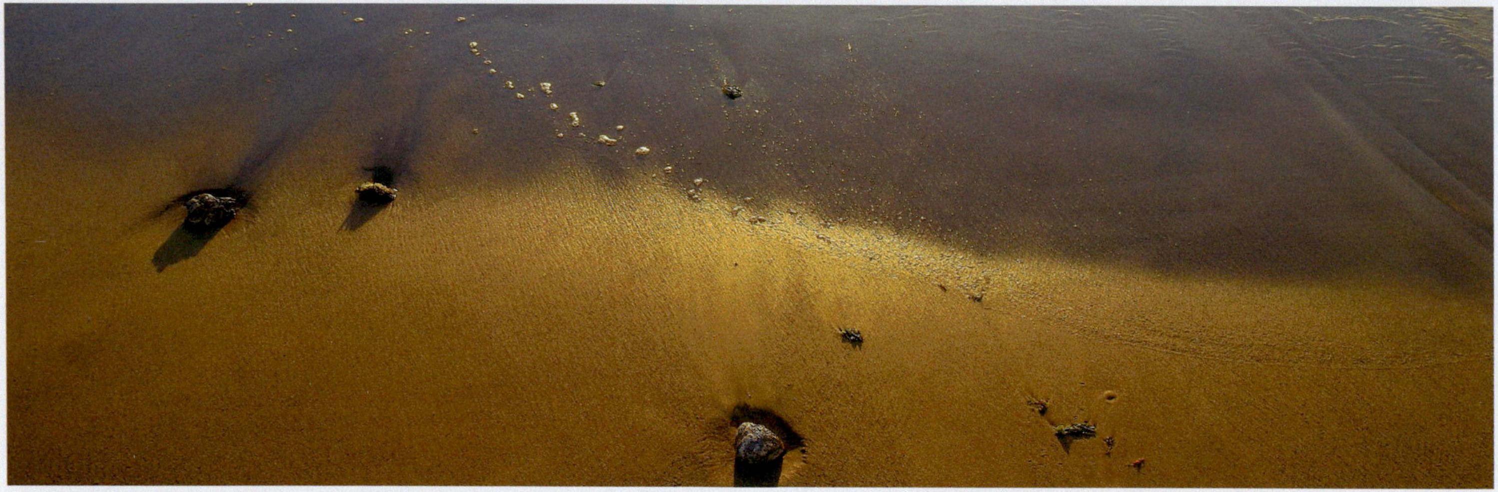

Becoming

Becoming
Always becoming

Becoming while listening
Becoming while doing

Always becoming

Becoming while sleeping
Becoming while receiving

Becoming is consciousness
Traveling through you

Becoming
Always becoming

Along with the stars in the sky
Along with the sand in the sea

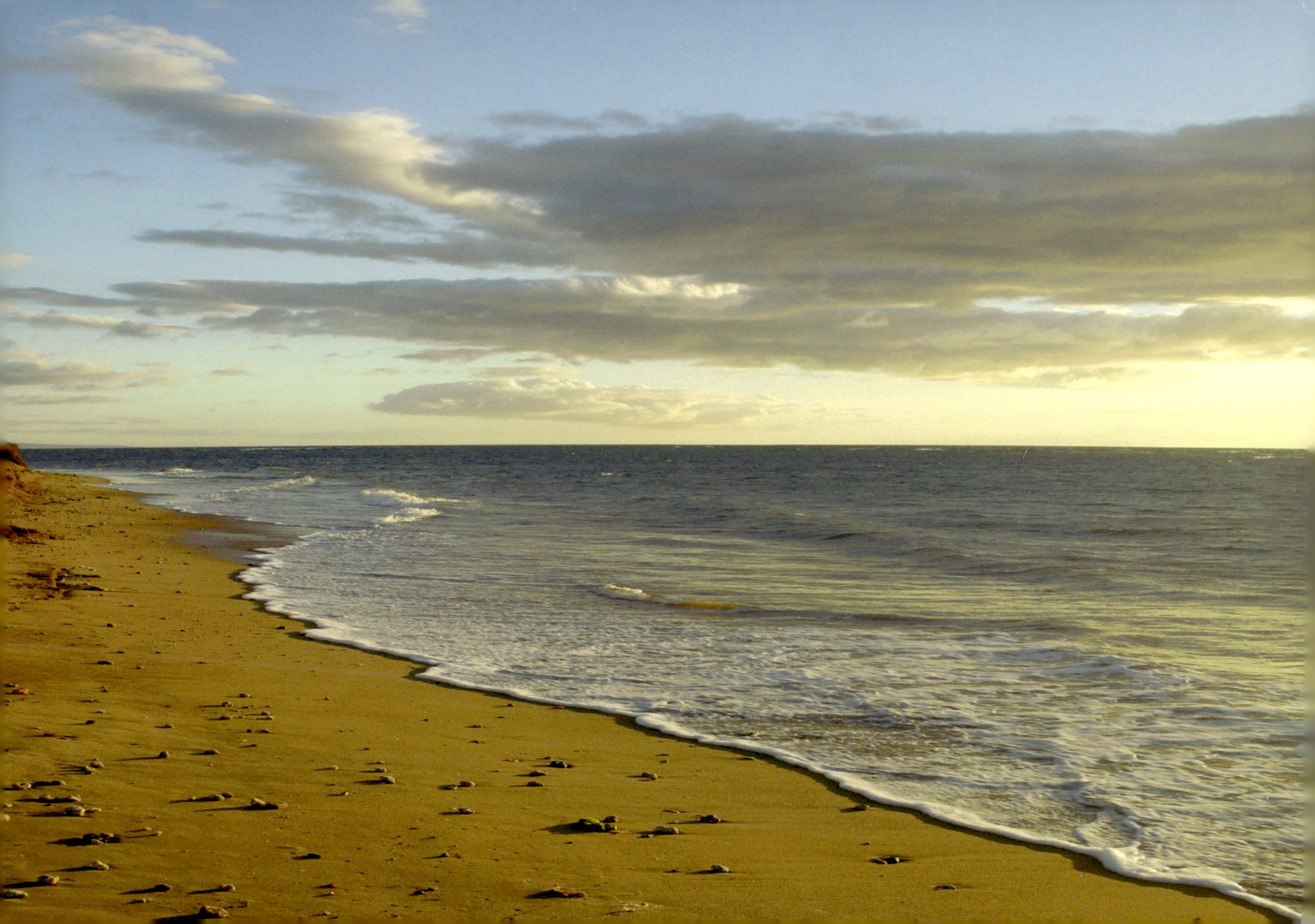

Expanded Ways

Even ultimately is expanding
Holdouts also expand
It has been no other way
Consciousness makes itself

Projection upon projection
Protection upon protection

Always manifesting
Me you them
In expansion
Ad infinitum

An alliance with expansion
Stretches the heart

Contain more
Hold more
Everything always expanding
How much can be held?

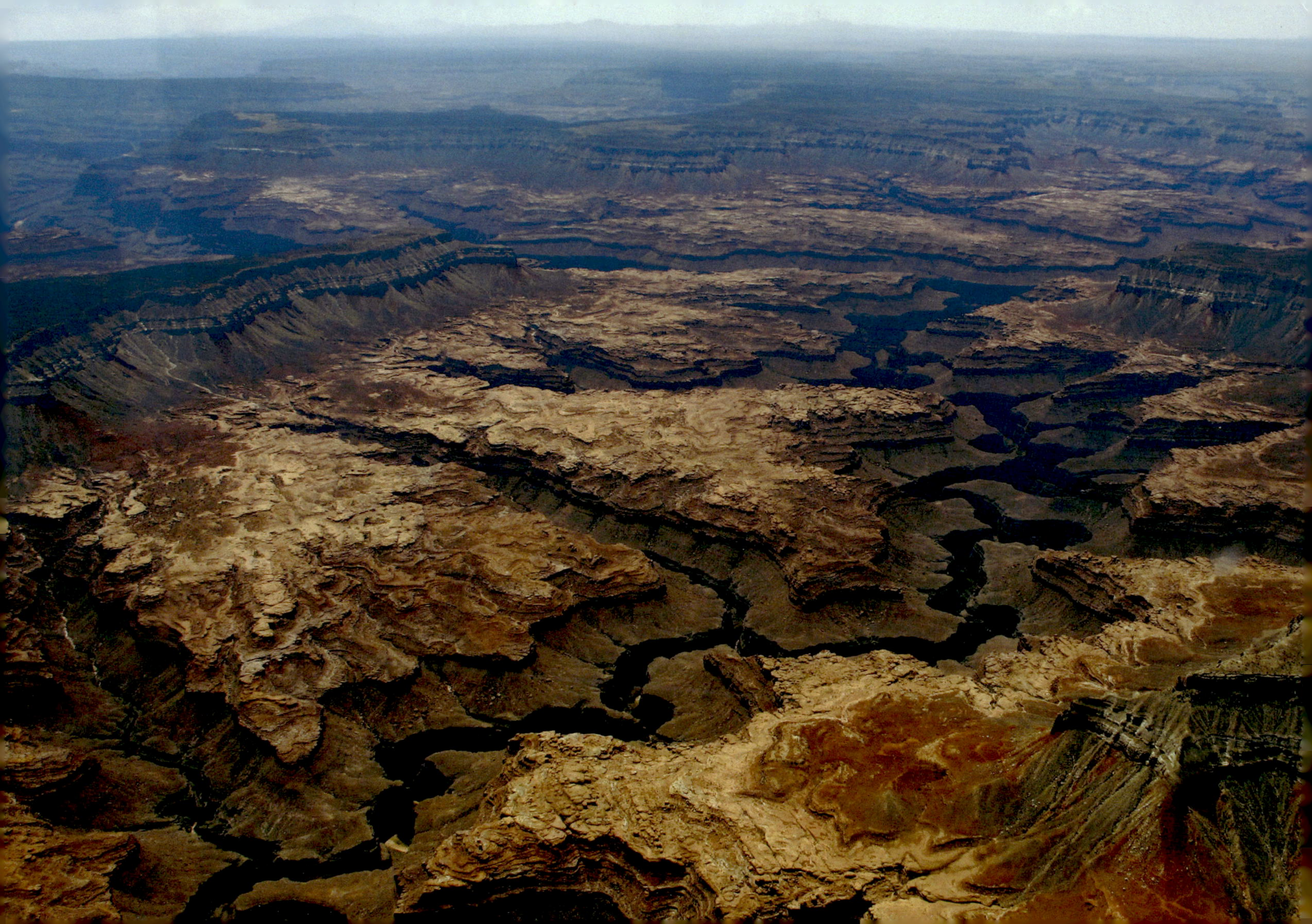

My Camera

My camera is my secret life
My inner world
Fog on a window
Lovers on a beach
Whatever the whim or impulse
Snap away

Wrong focus or
Bright spots are
After thoughts
To the fun of pressing the shutter

Long exposures are the best
Waiting for the capturing
Waiting for the processing
Waiting for the surprise
From inside looking out

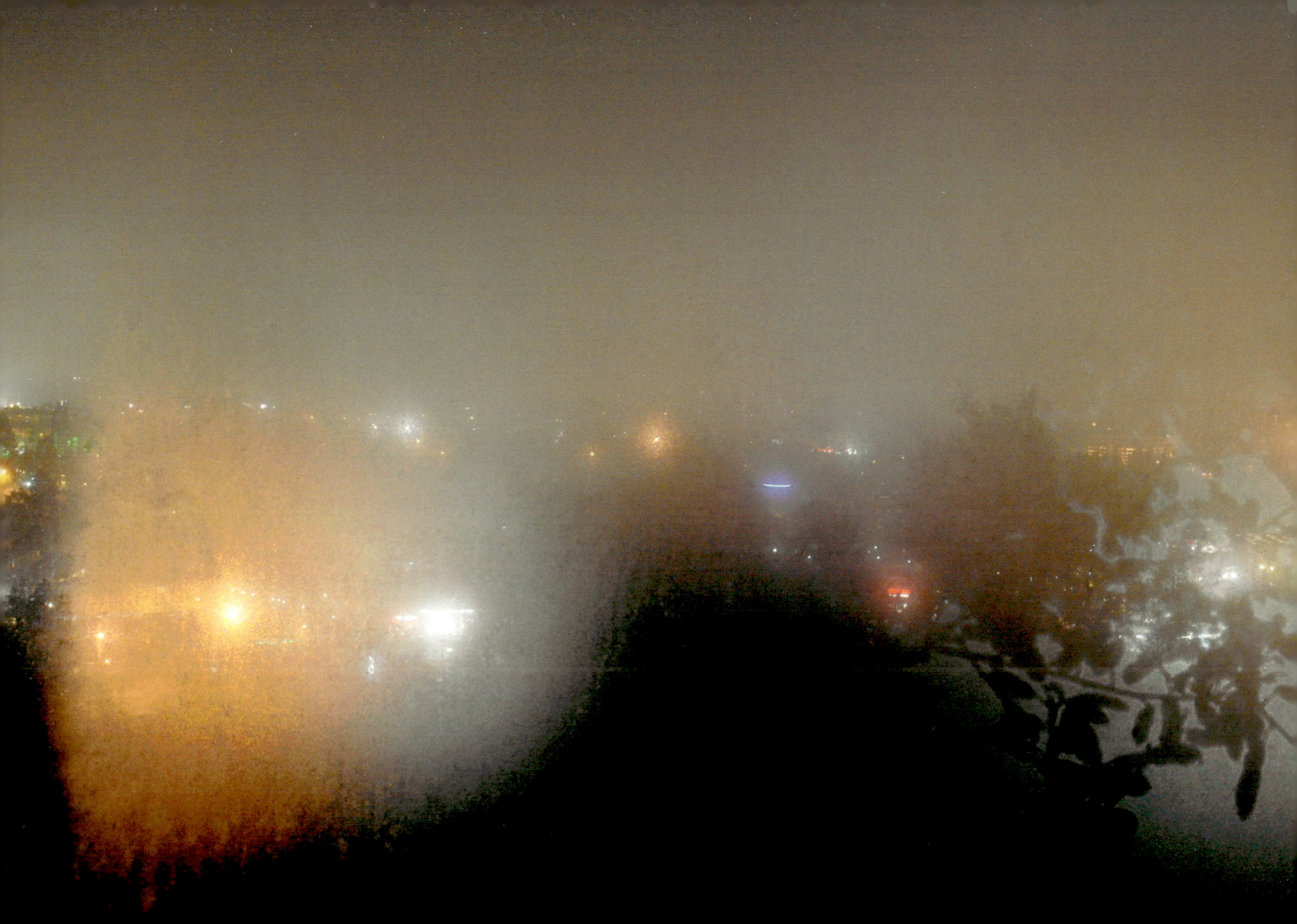

Feeds My Eyes

To see out
I sit in the dark

The view feeds my eyes
With mist in the purple mountains

An eternal enchantment

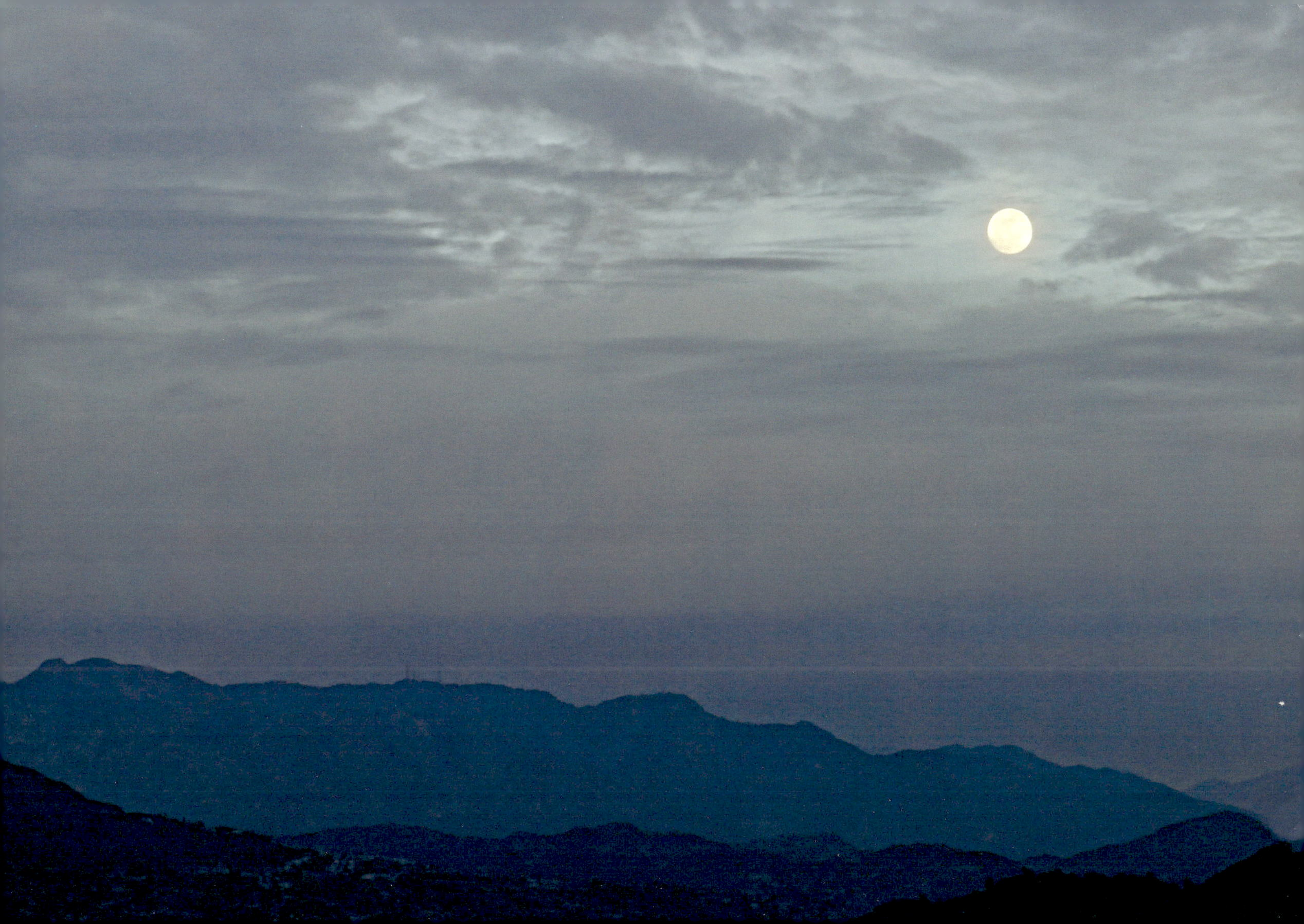

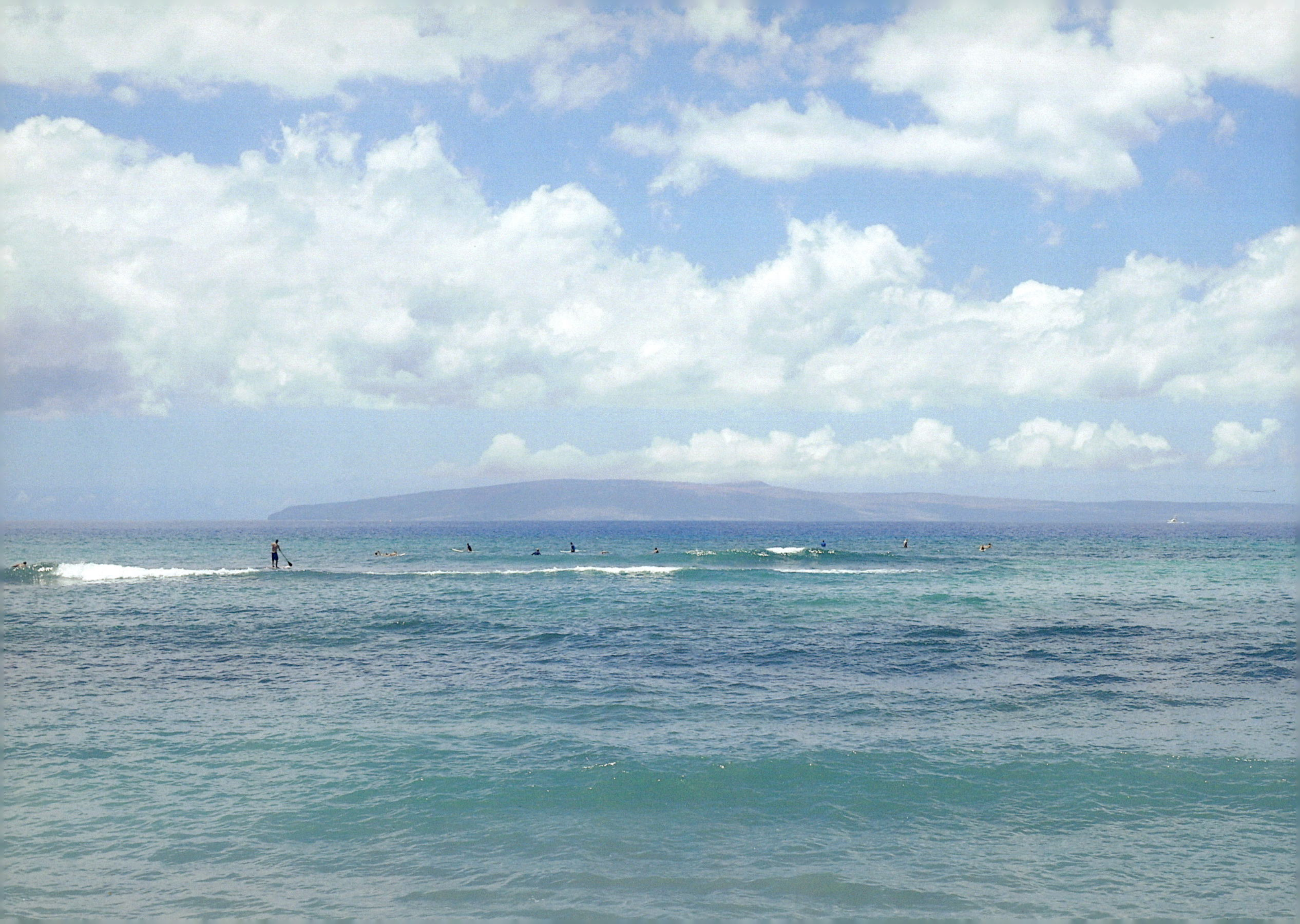

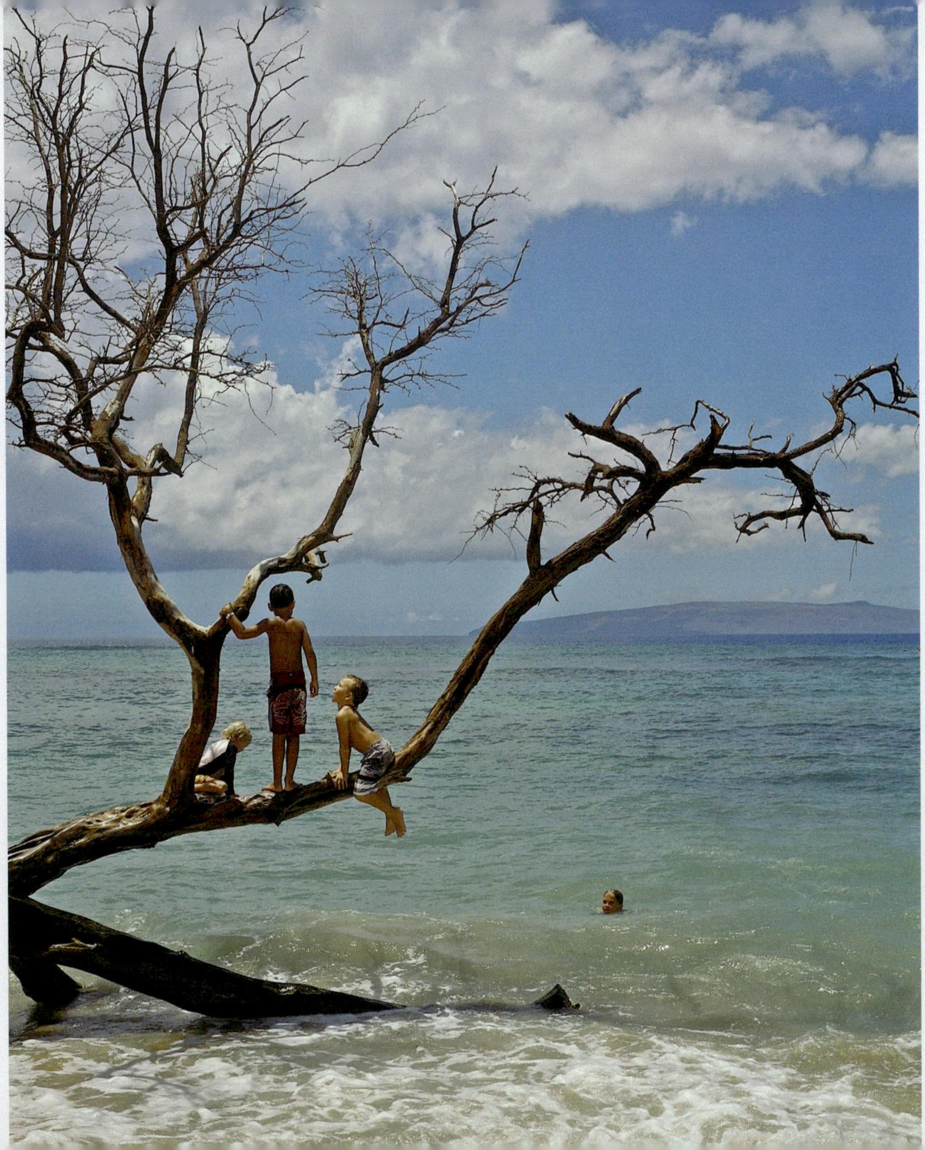

Eagerness

In co-creation
Making a choice
Makes a voice
The expanding unmanifest
Comes through
Make a choice
Open the floodgates
For all tomorrows
Sit on a fence
Enjoy the view
As long as you want to
As long as you have to
Lifetimes times ten
Then when you want
When you want enough
To be eager
Make a choice
Eagerness as a mistress
Imagination as a guide
Ah today's choices

For You

The more you want
The more the Universe dreams
For you

The more you dream
The more the Universe wants
For you

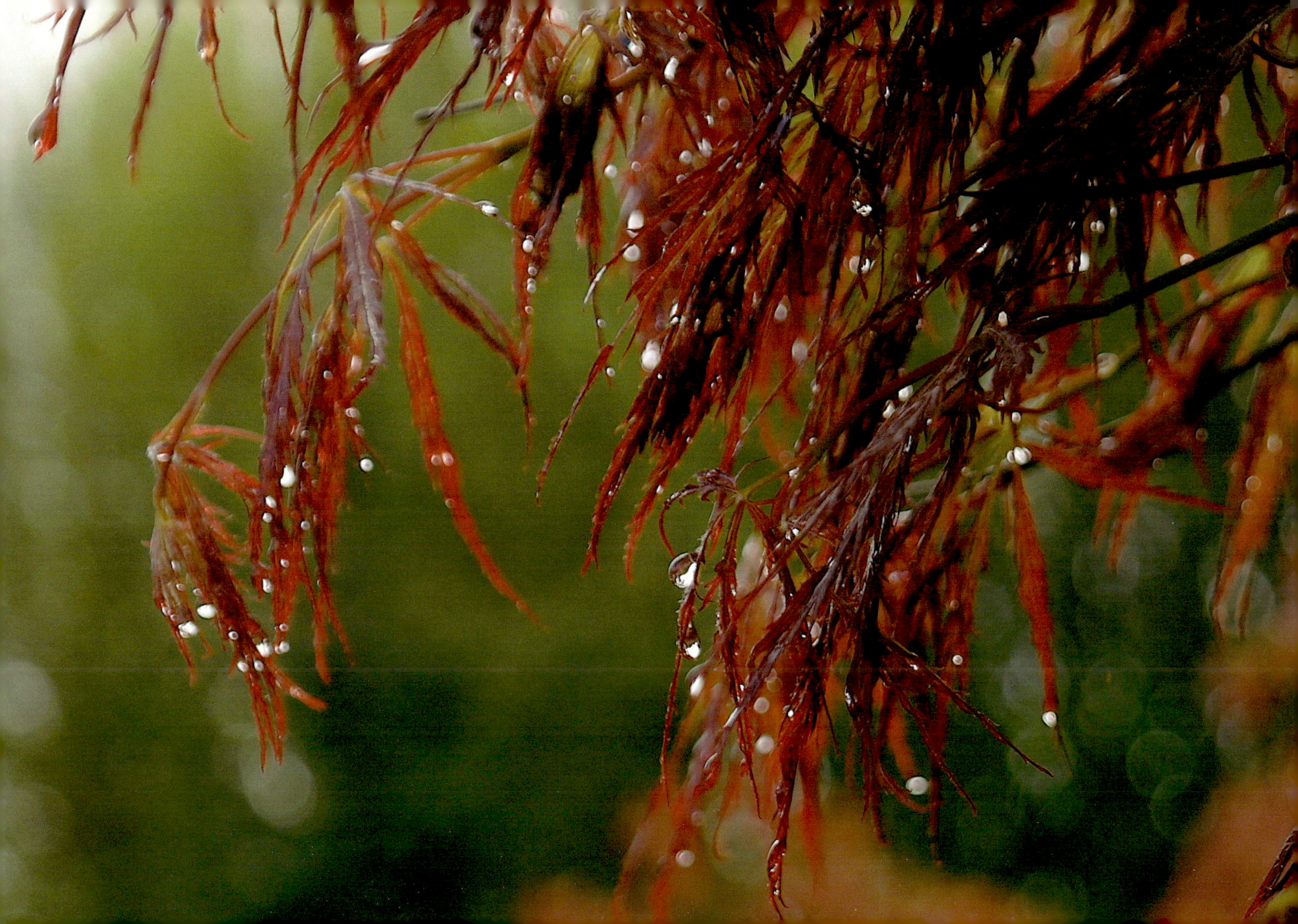

Hear a New Life for Yourself

How can you hear new life for yourself?
Pay attention to your very cells
Know the moment the skin starts to burn
This is awareness
Awareness from the inside out

If you are not curing
Change
If you like white
Start liking blue
If you like quiet
Accept noise

Break up the patterns that make you sick
It takes attention to shift
To make yourself well
To hear a new life for yourself

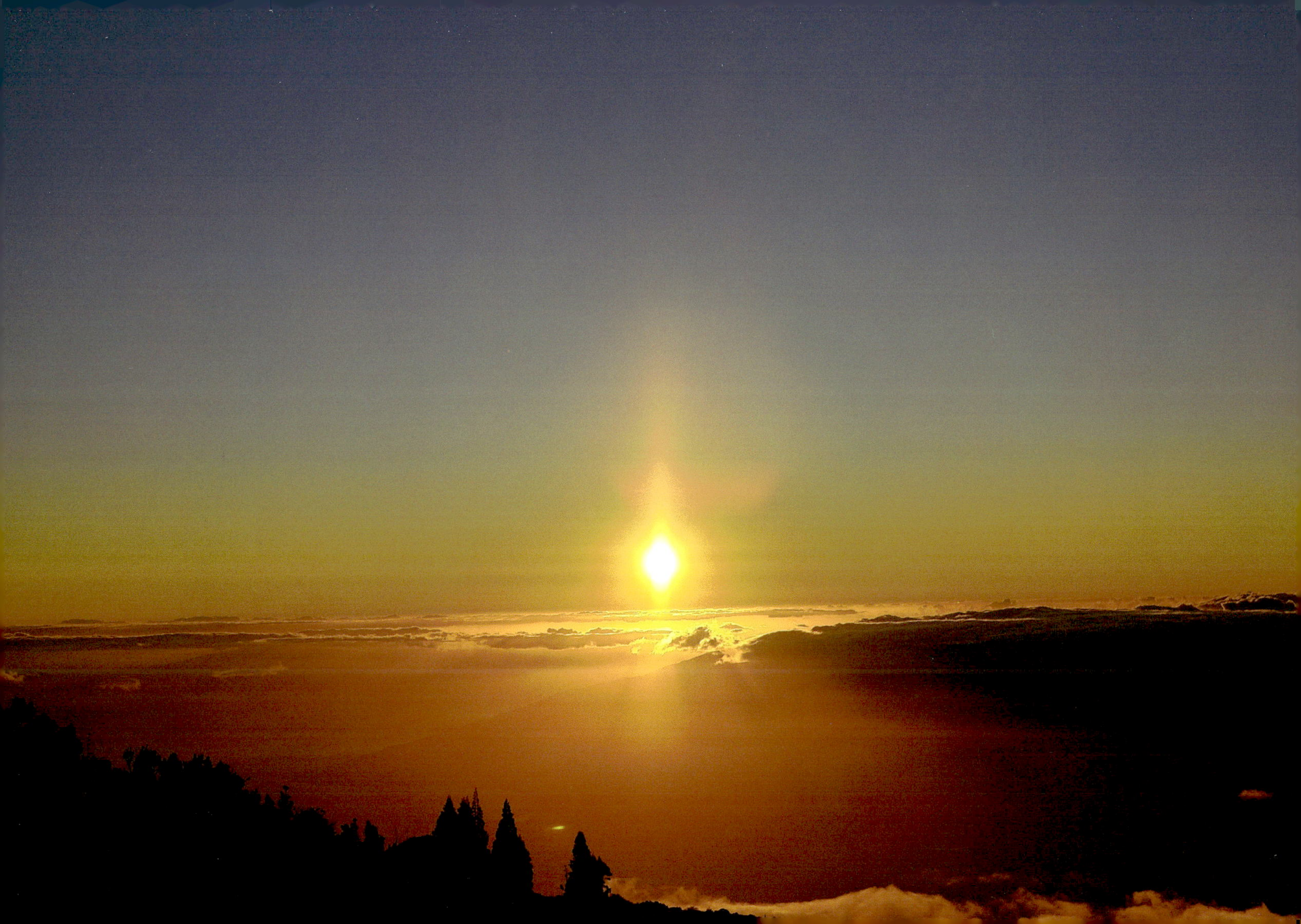

How to Find Your Bliss

When you get a tingle
In every cell of your being
Inside and outside
Is it excitement, fear or bliss?

So many rivers of light
Carry the timeless boundless current
It is so much
It is too much
We throw up resistance

We cannot flow as much ever
As there is flowing
Always current flowing
Always resistance

Find your bliss
Flowing through your veins
By lowering your resistance to it

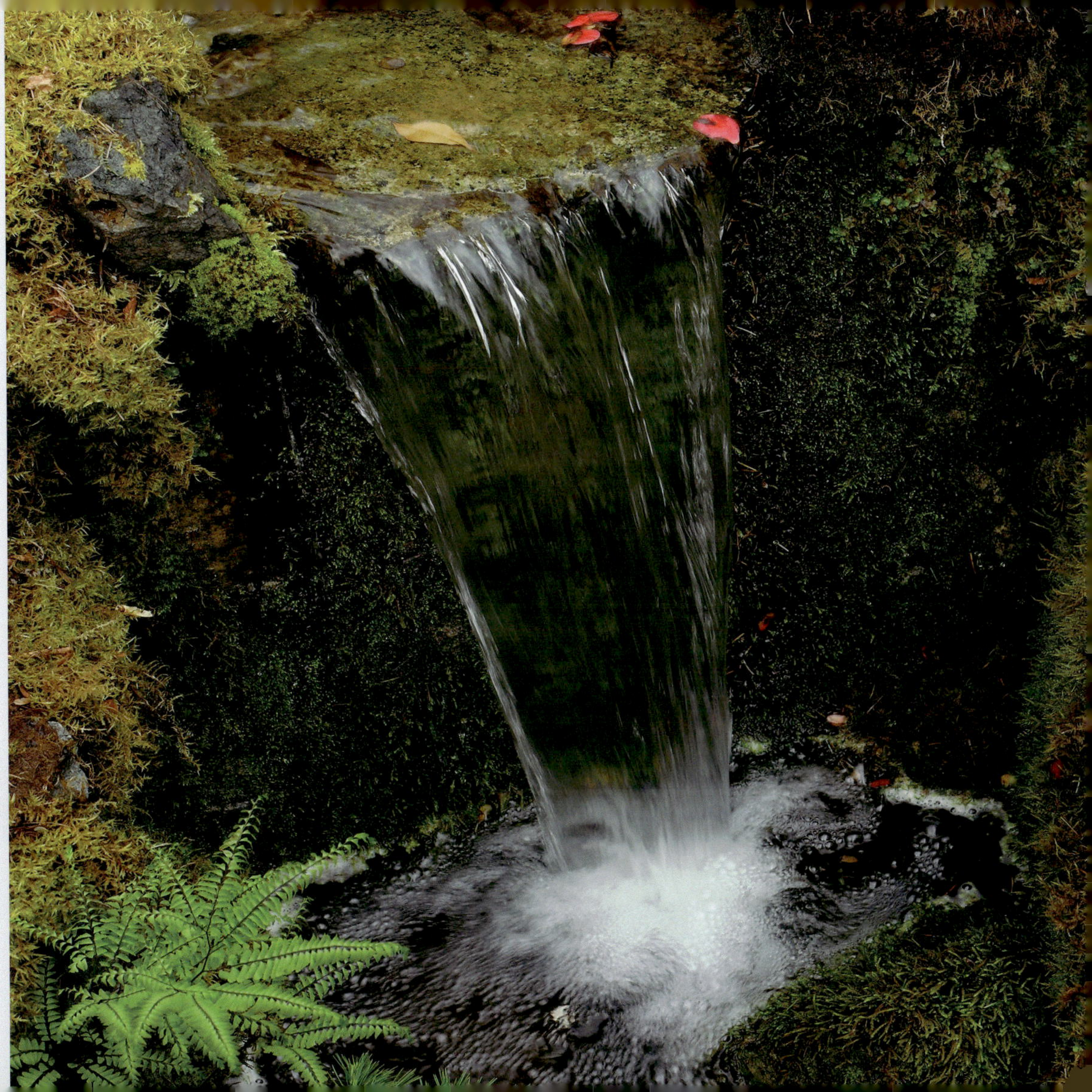

Hold a Kitten

I am holding a kitten
Holding a kitten
To know what love feels like

I am open to ribbons of light
I am open to being more
I am open to the future
To eons of creation
Swirling chaos
Mystery and magic

Petting this kitten
Opening the gateways of love

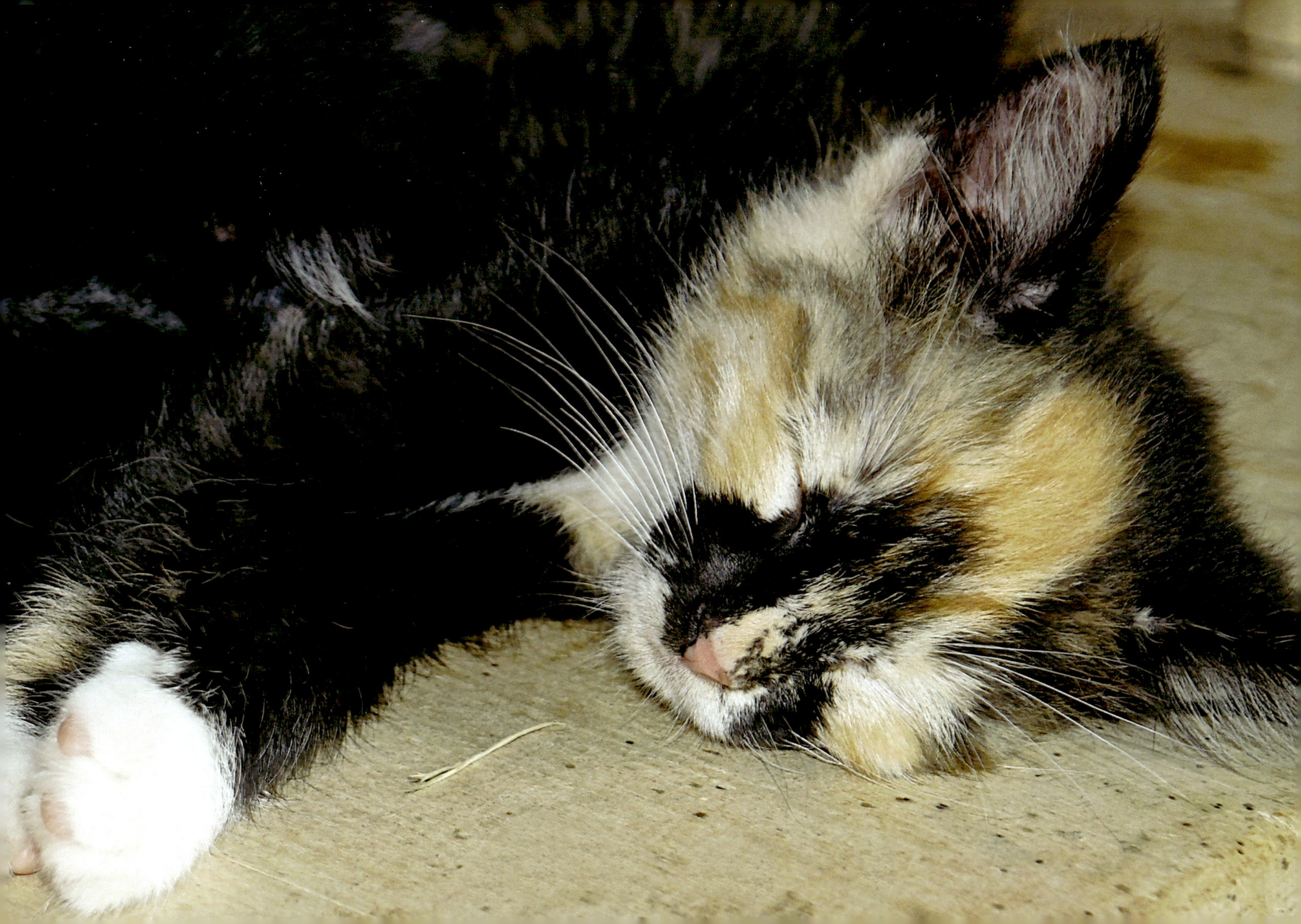

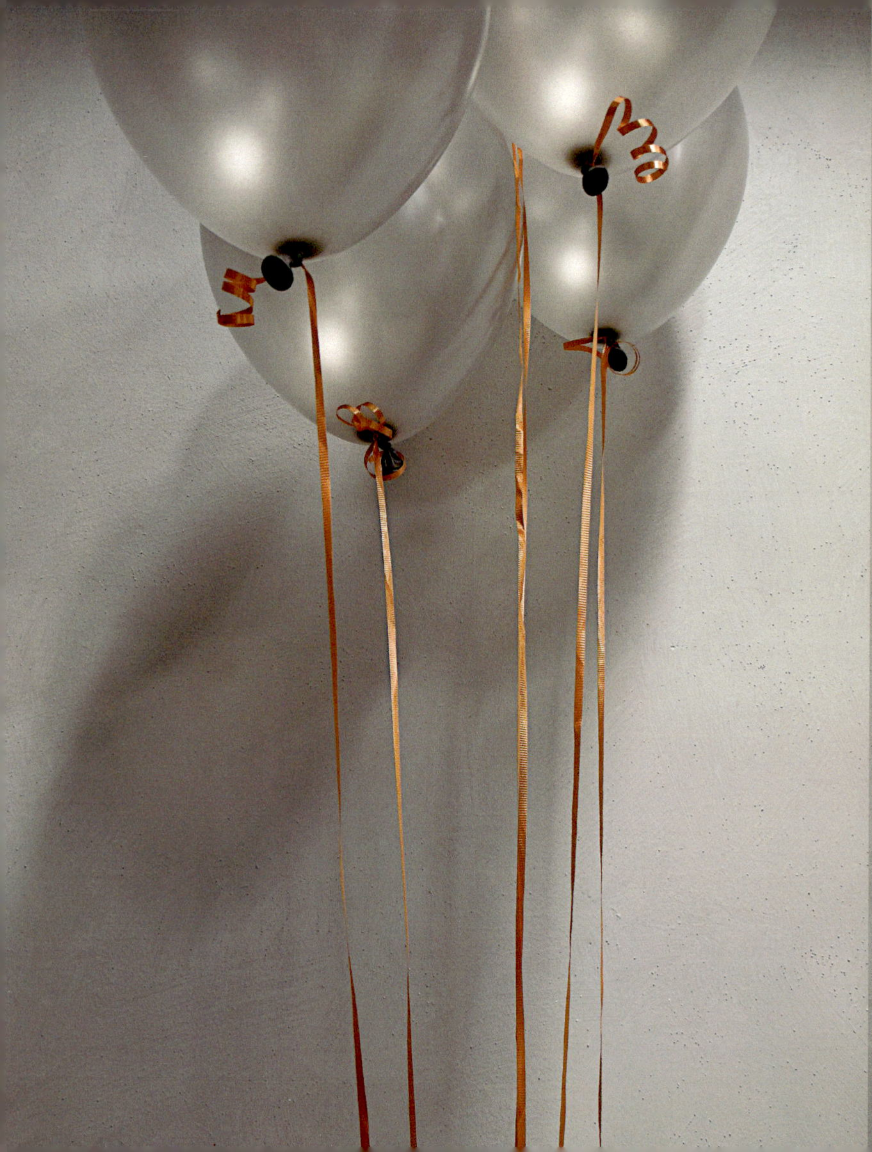
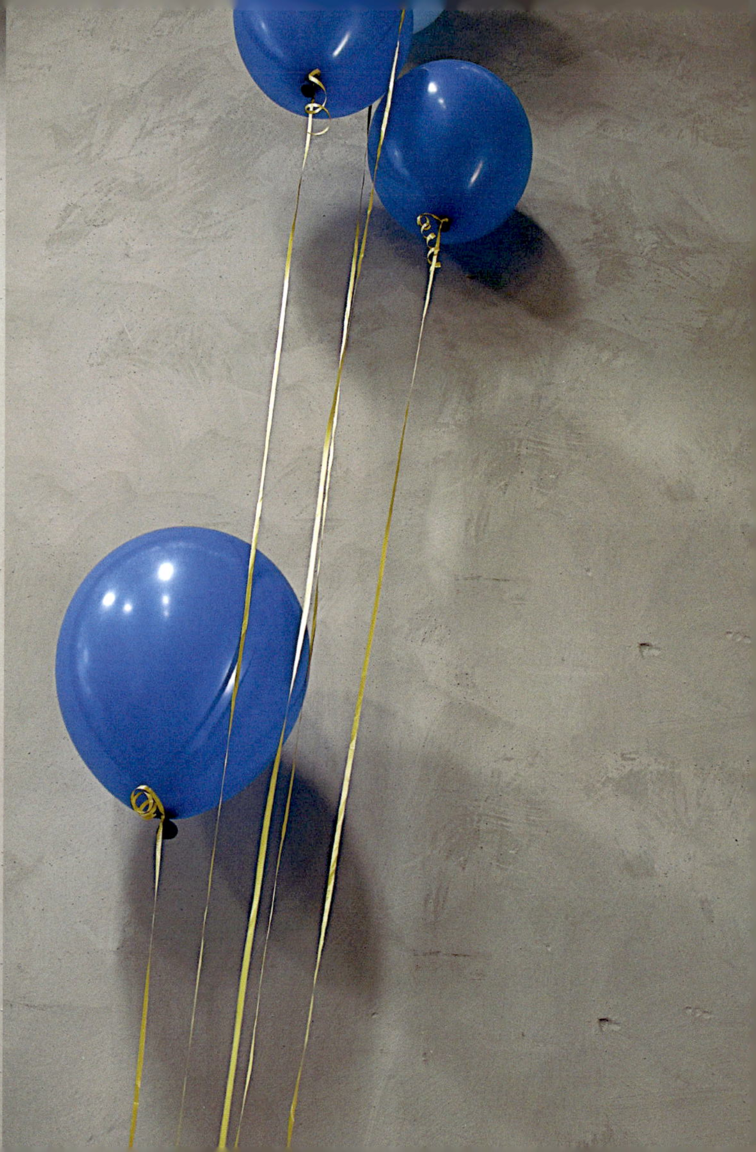

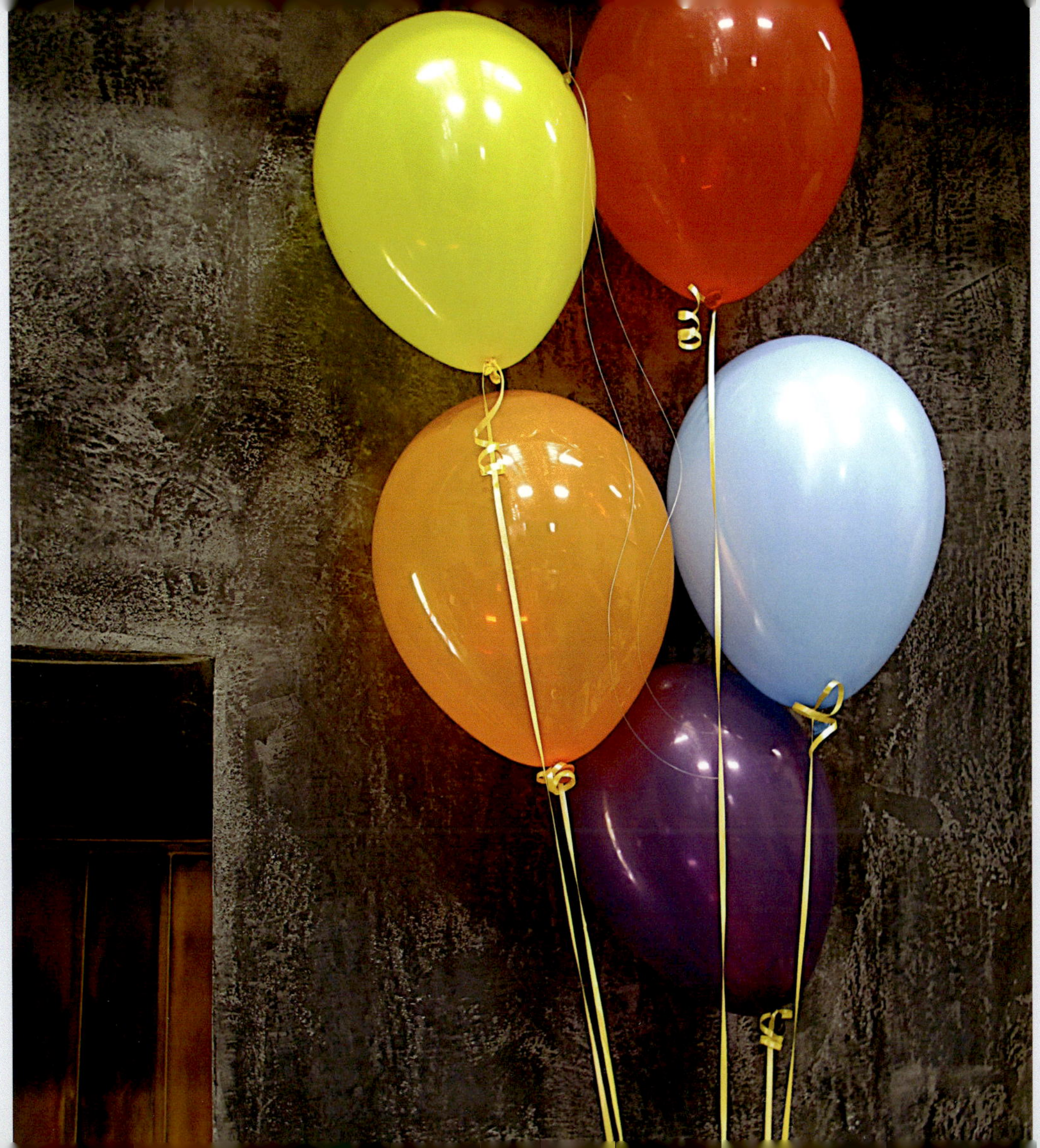

Fun

It's going to be fun
Remembering past fun
Imagining future fun

I hold the full feeling of fun
While I am eating or
Brushing my hair

It is my choice
I choose fun

Expectancy and Receiving

Don't expect what you can't receive
Make room if you expect
Celebrate its coming
Receiving

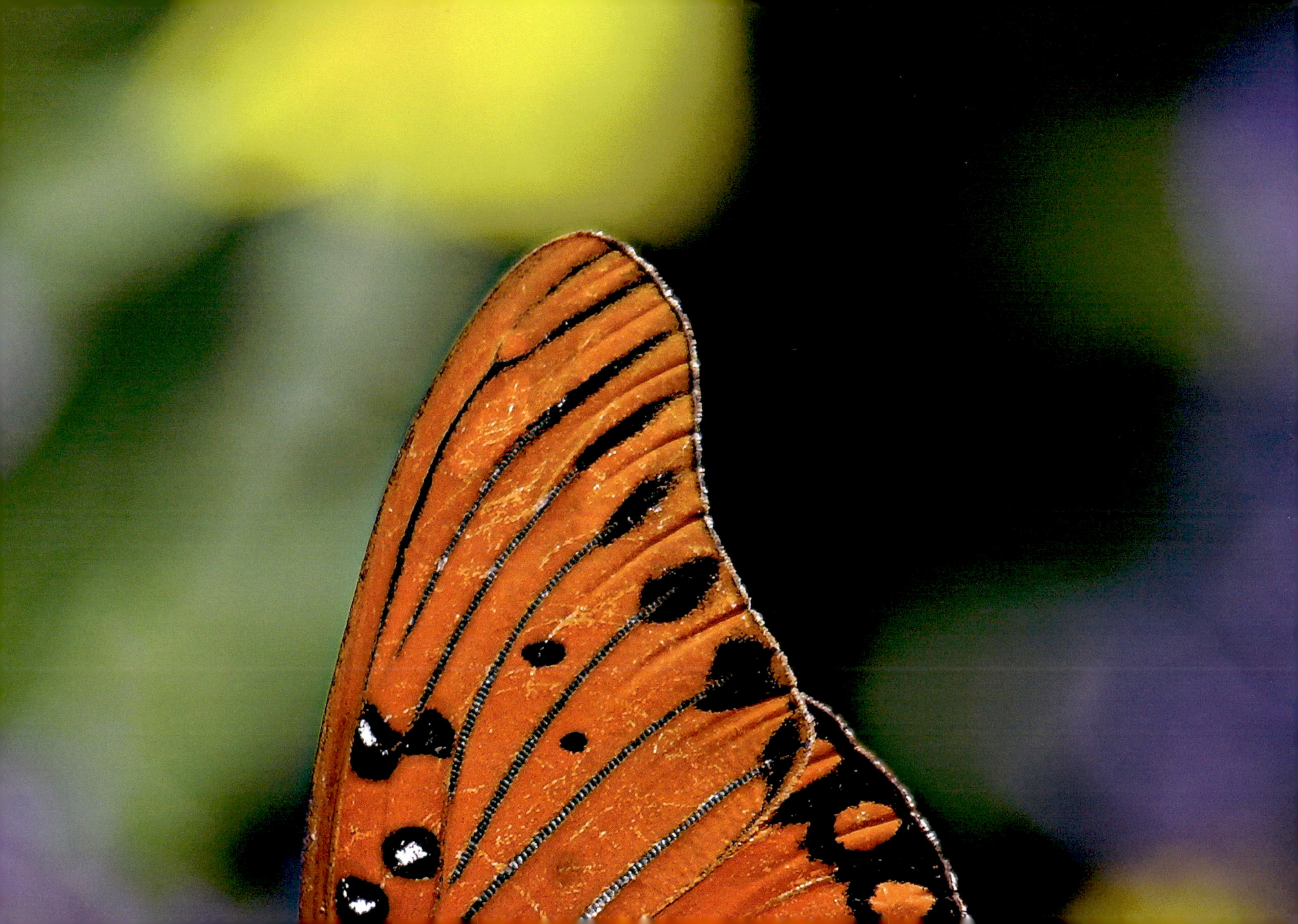

Camera

First years with a camera
You take what the camera
Sees

Next years with a camera
You take what the viewer
Sees

Later years with a camera
You take what your eye
Sees

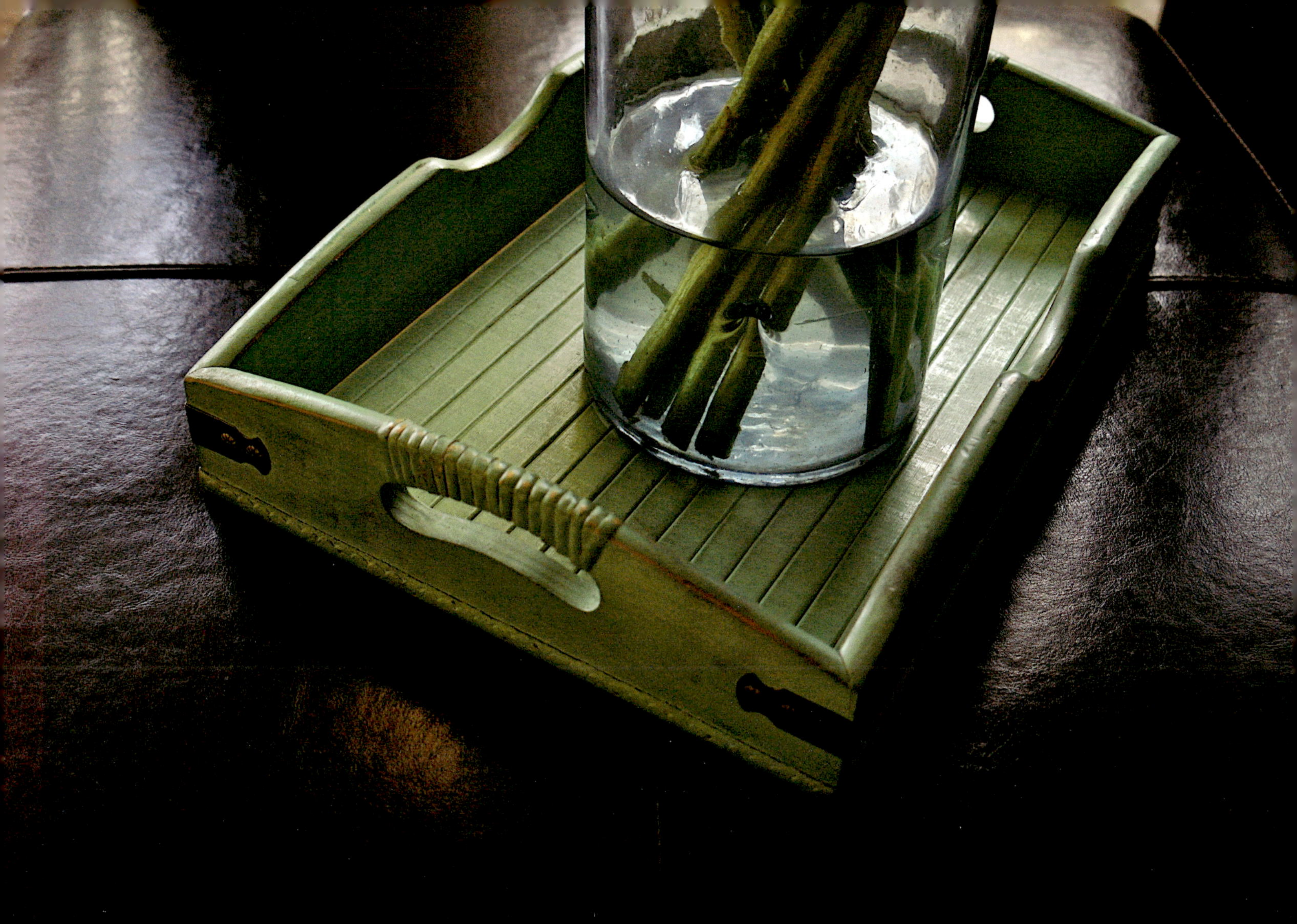

My Bounty

My bounty is having
Lilacs in the house
They make the heart sing

Do I like them?
Yes they are so easy to like
Ah affection
A warm and wonderful feeling
So easy to come by

You don't have to like lilacs
That's the good part
But you like something
That's your bounty

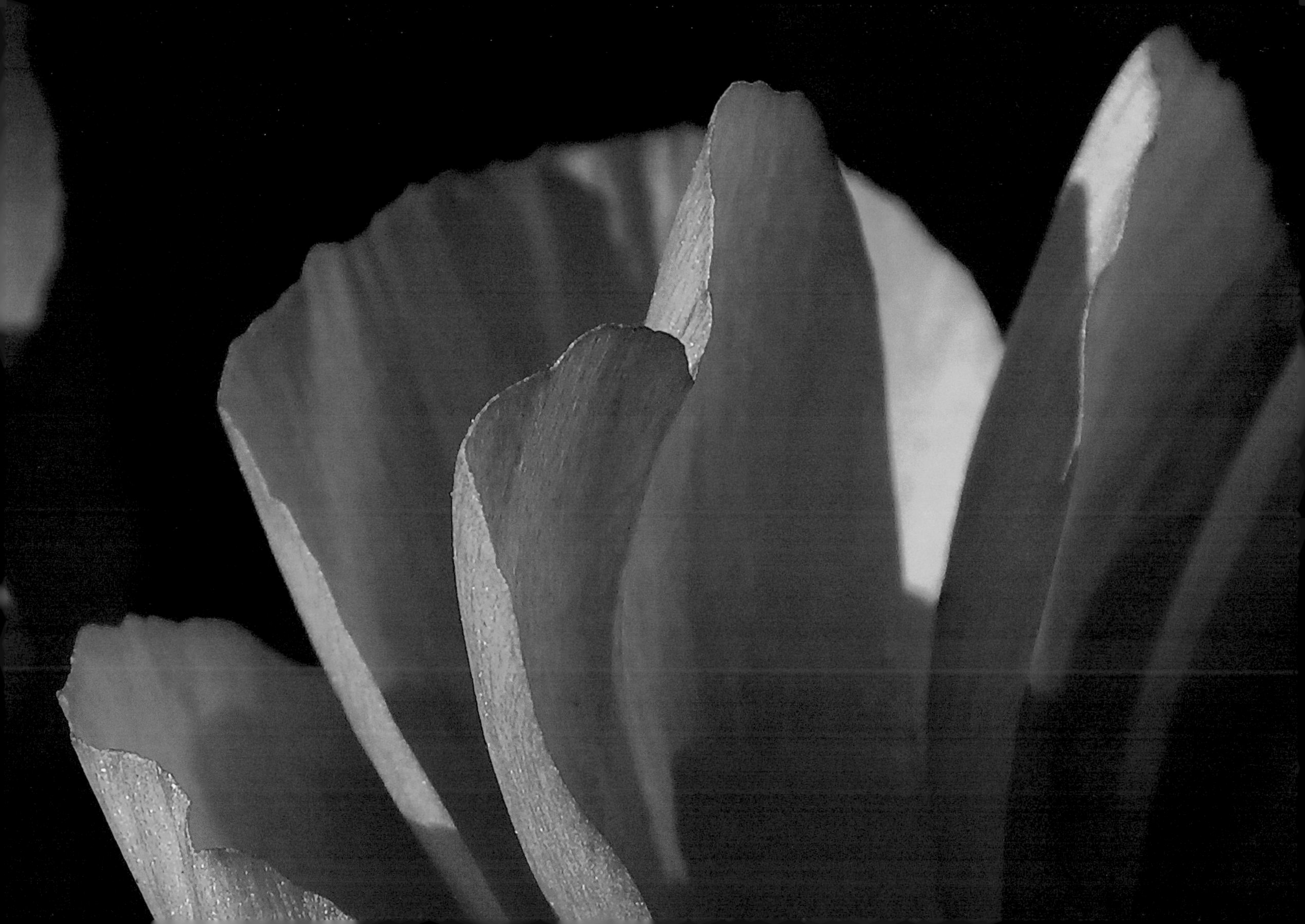

My Buddy

How warm kitty's ears
When it's cold outside
And he's sitting here with me

He wraps both front feet in at the center
And leans his head over for stroking
This is a very precious moment

His silky ears so alluring
His silken fur our illusion

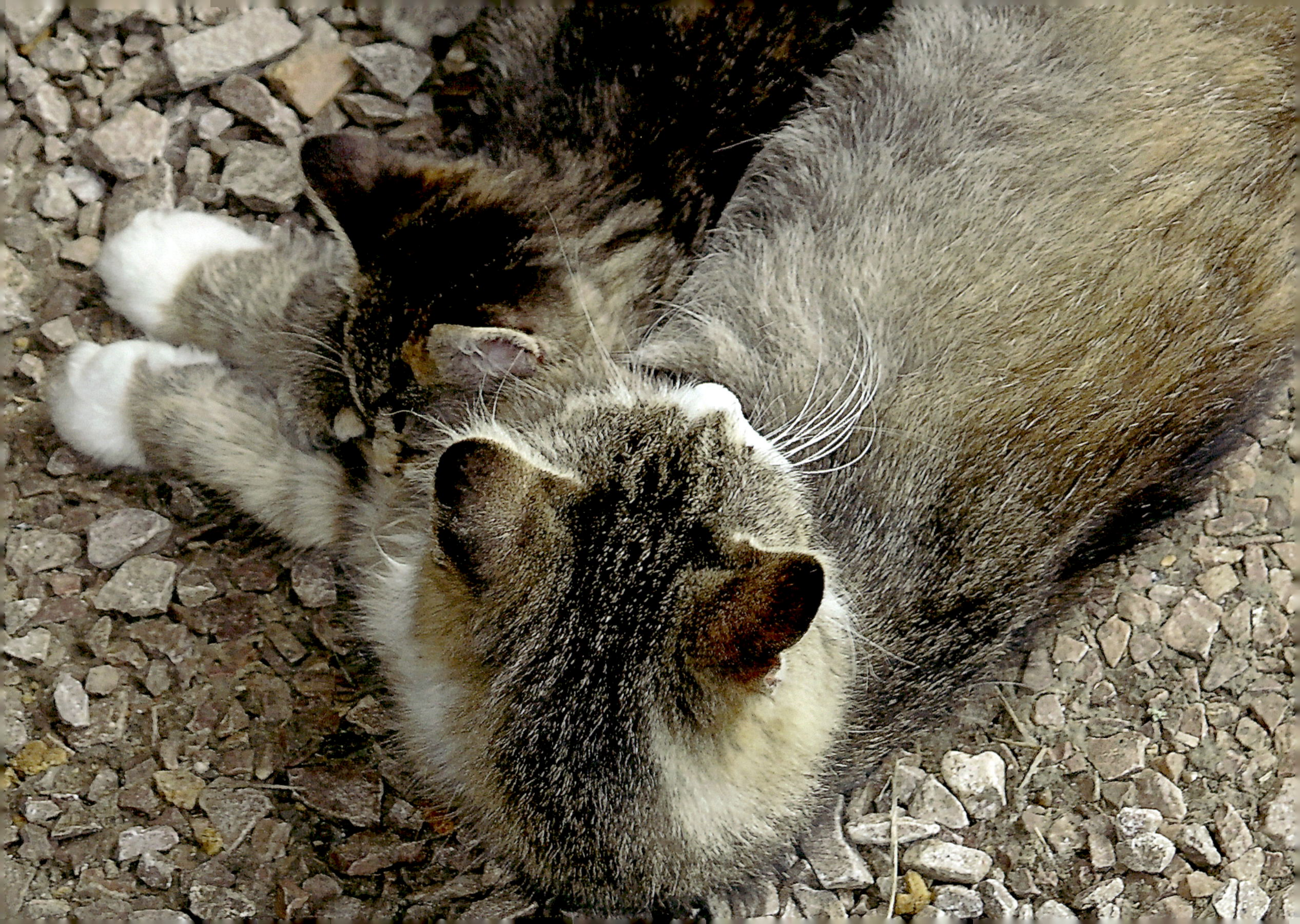

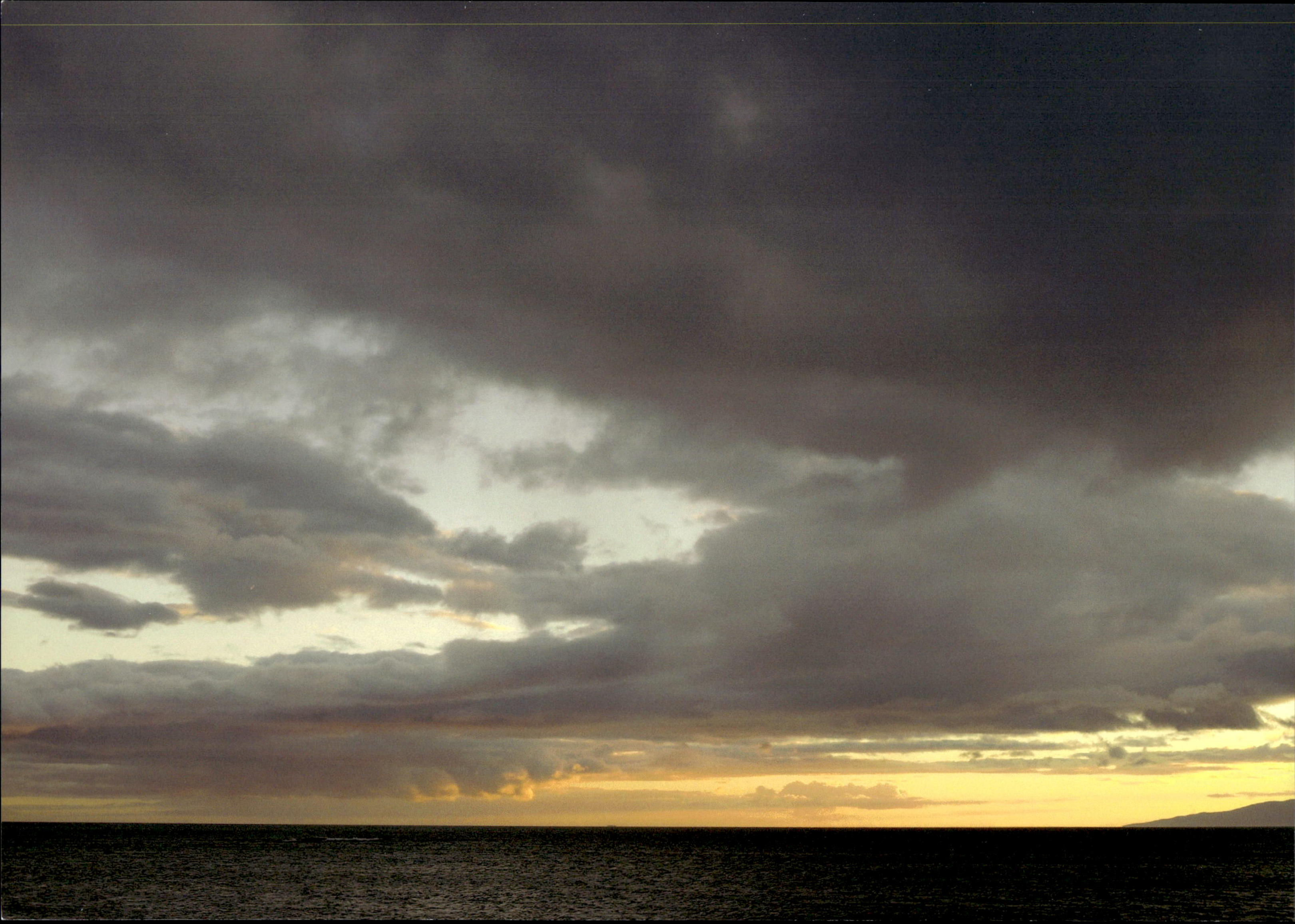

I Allow

As a flowing belief
As a co-creator
I am bringing life into the illusion

Allowing my heart to desire
Allowing my mind to imagine
Allowing myself to expect
Helps the unmanifest manifest
In directions I can allow

I encourage myself to allow more
I allow myself more
        more and more
        endless more

My allowing contributes
        to next week
        to next year
        to next lifetime

Co-creating with the unmanifest
My contribution to tomorrow

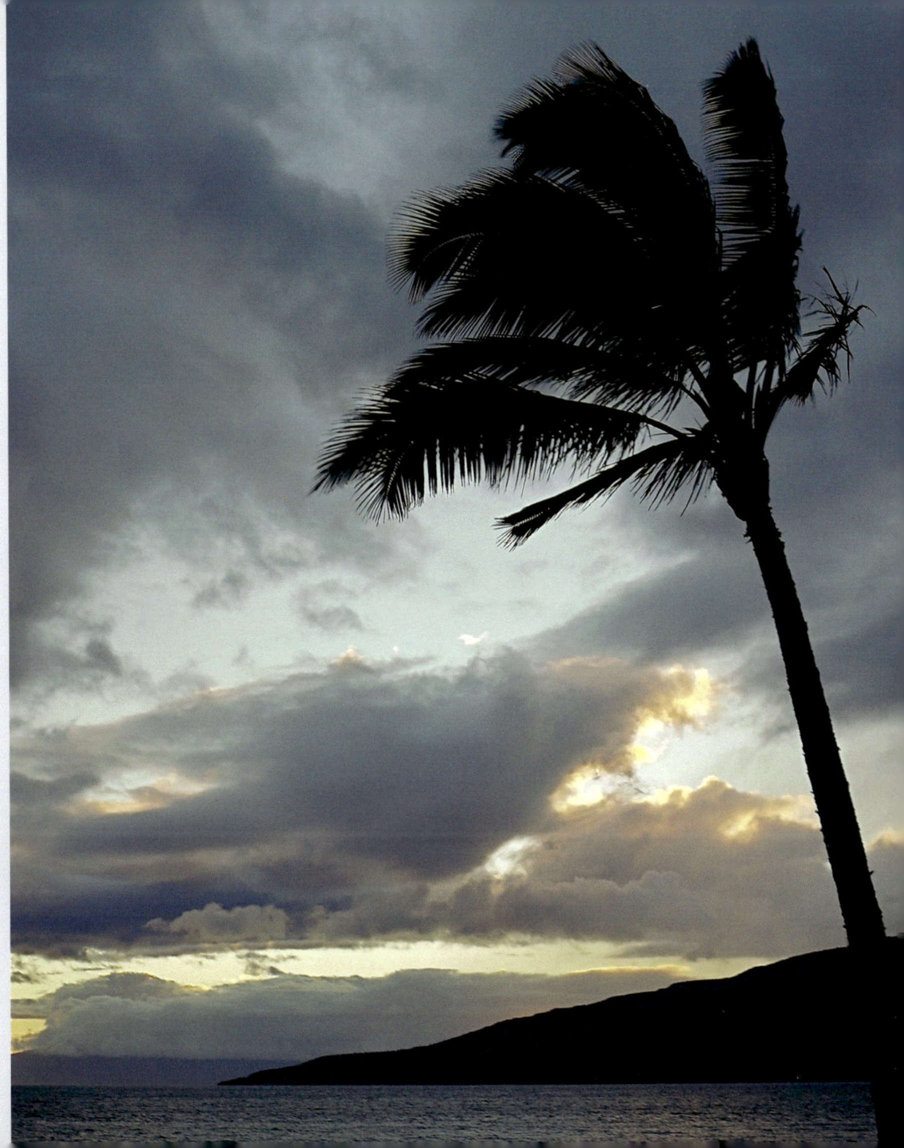

My Camera Says

My camera says capturing
Then it says processing
Capturing/processing

Is capturing an aggressive word?
For co-creation that's what it takes

Grab the light
Pull the light in
Capture it

Is processing an arduous word?
For co-creation that's what it takes

Digest the light
Saturate the light
Process it

My camera captures and processes
With such ease

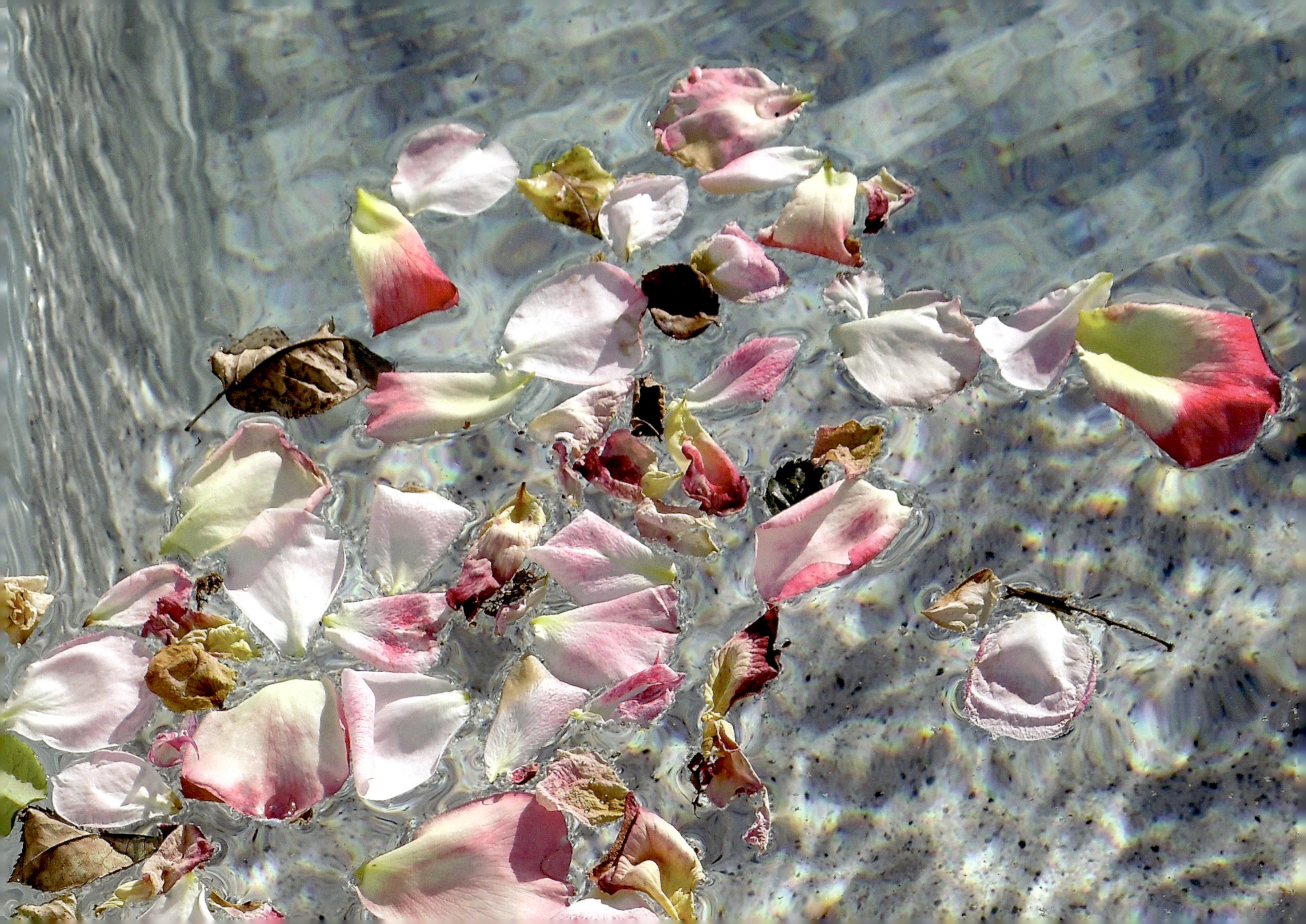

Fall in Love

How can you fall in love with something
You don't admit to having?

How can you fall in love with something
That has so much power over you?

Something that says
When you will live and when you will die

Nevertheless
Fall in love with your soul

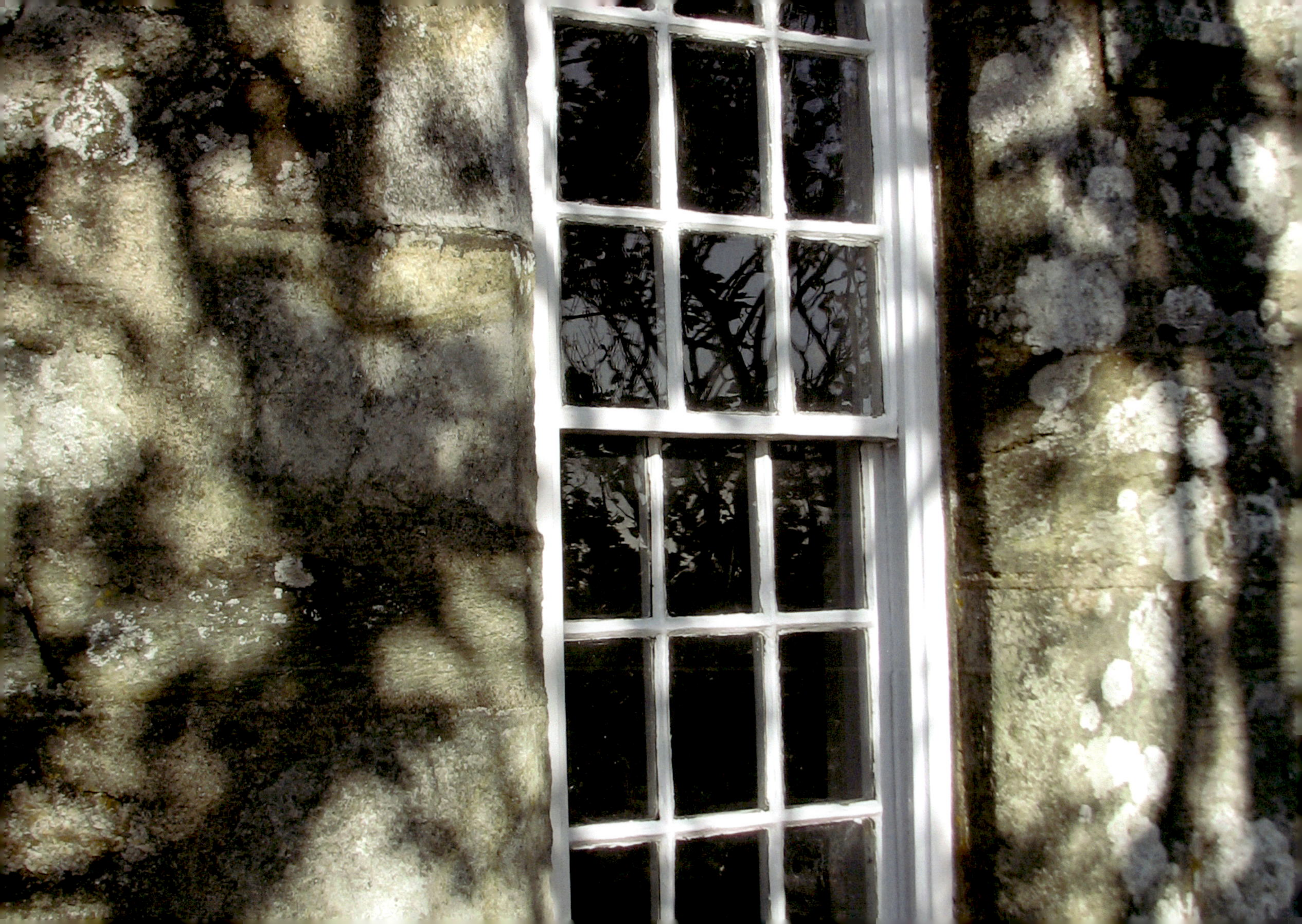

Not Afraid

I have seen light and shadow
So many times now
I don't need my camera
I need the light
Always changing light

I have seen dark and light
So many times now
I am no longer afraid

The dark is a master of change
How long will it take
Until I trust
Until I trust
That I can turn around in the dark
Lighten it shade by shade
Until it is past light gray

As the light fades
My camera needs to open more
To capture more light
I need to do the same

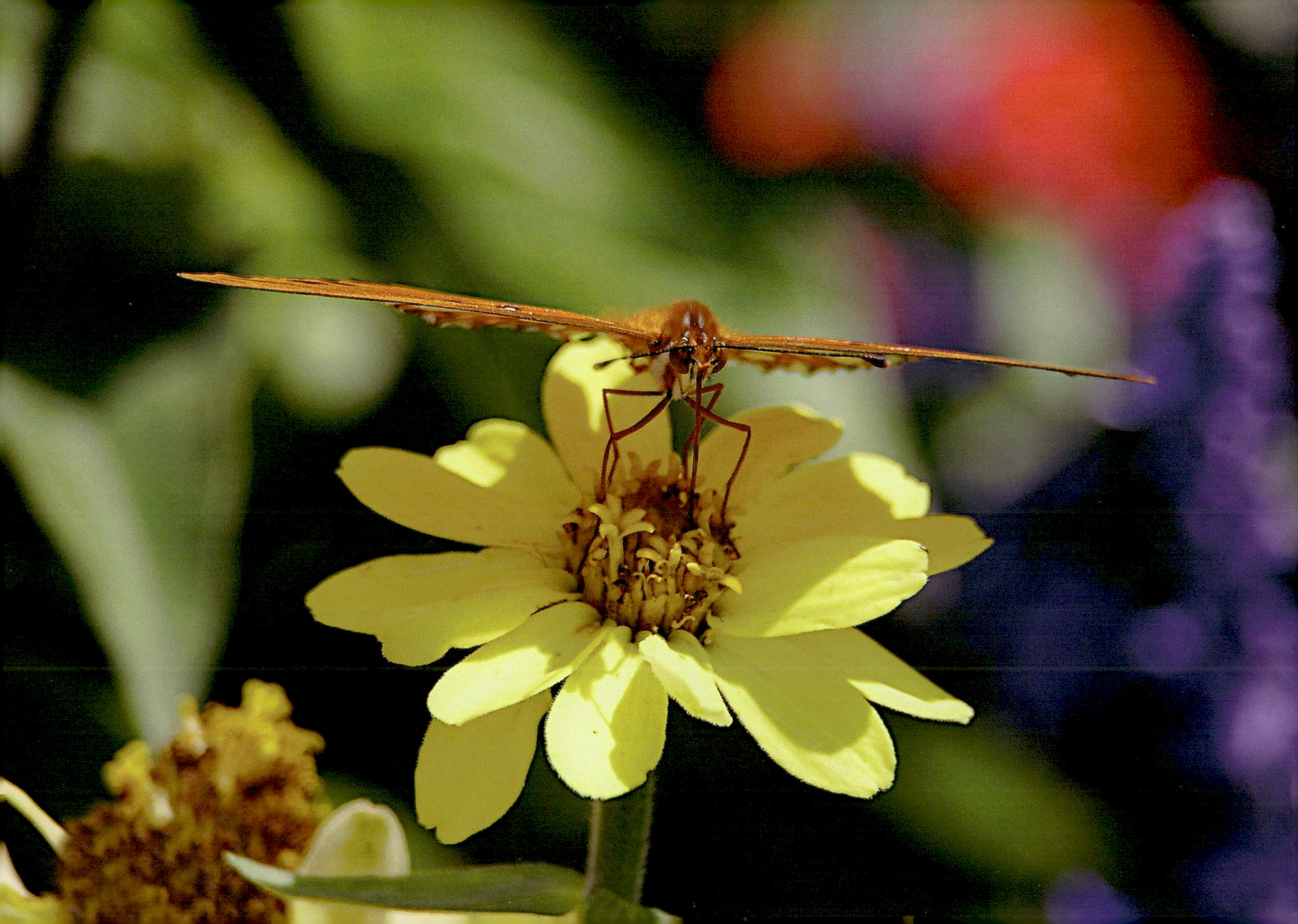

Open to the Unknown

Open to the unknown parts of yourself
Yes it is unknown
But it is you

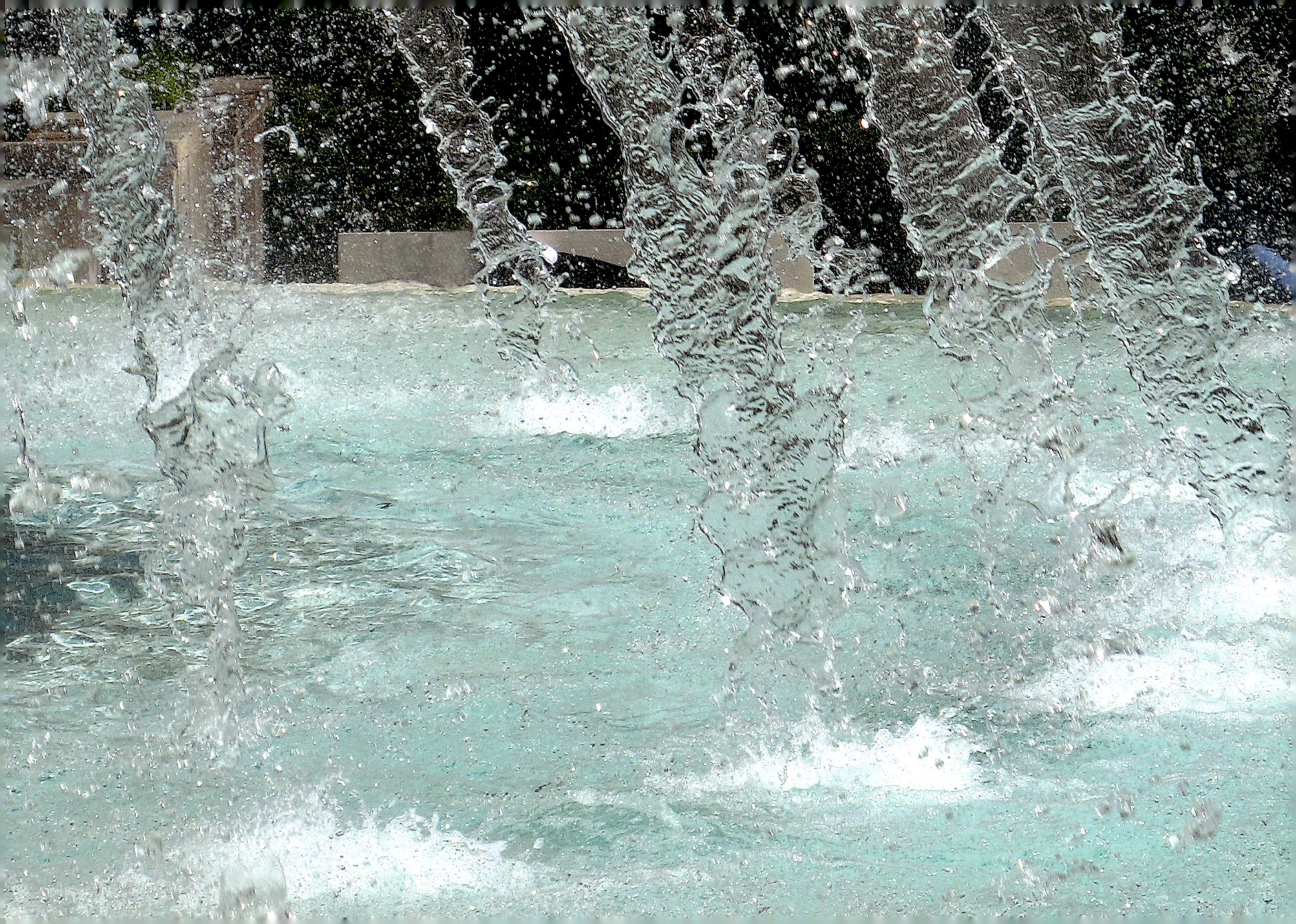

Soaring to Manifestation

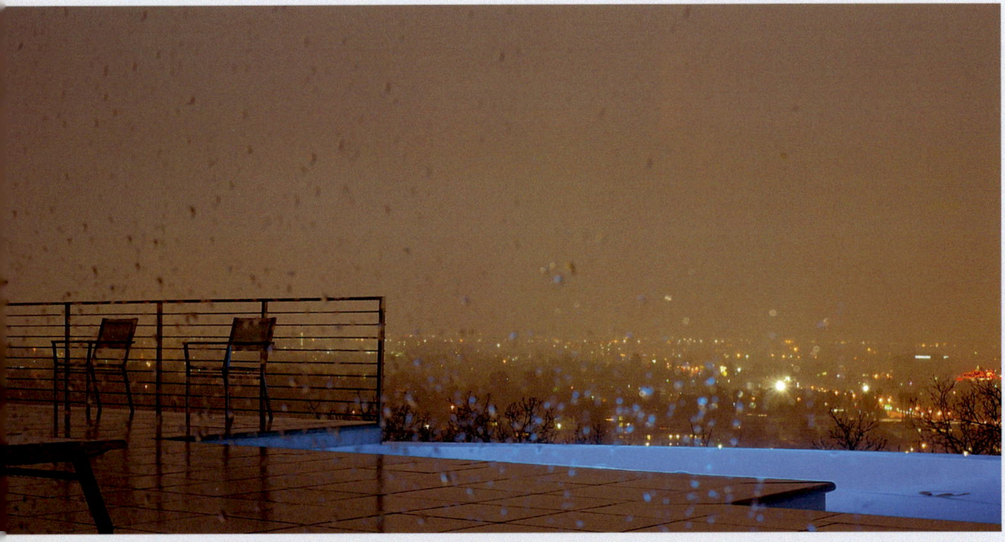

To swim
We go in
To manifest
We go in and out

Going into mystery
There a balloon to ride
Adding mysticism
Dancing too
Until intoxicated

Getting lifted
Getting gifted
Takes receiving
Opening the heart
Wide and full
Until swimming
On clouds

Now dream your dreams
Now manifest with ease

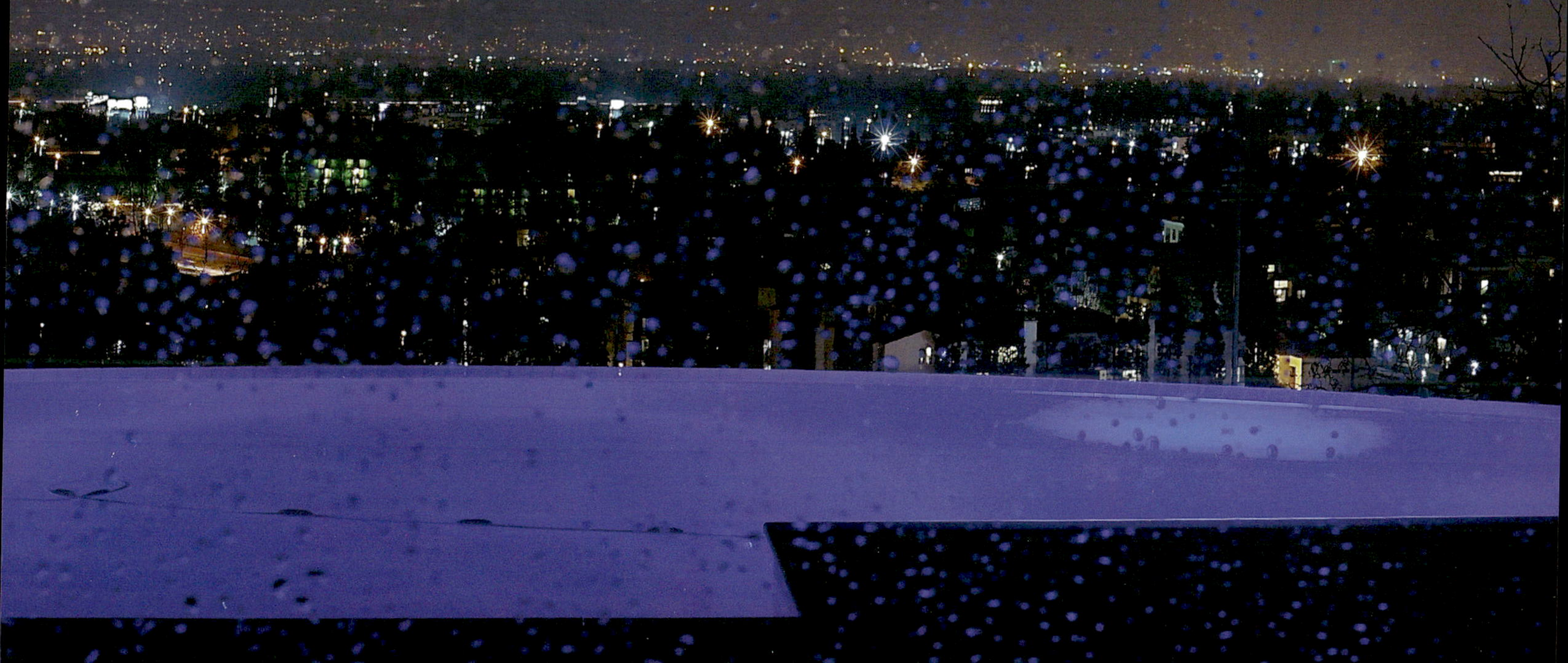

Three Crows

For a second of my experience
Three crows dance through the air

Wispy clouds let through some blue
Holding the hush in their vastness

The future is so full
How can I fear it?

Unfinished Work

Just how powerful
Is my soul?

If I cannot visualize my soul
Is it missing?

Remembering my soul never ceases
Helps take the fear out of connecting

So powerful my soul
Patiently waiting for me
To catch a glimpse

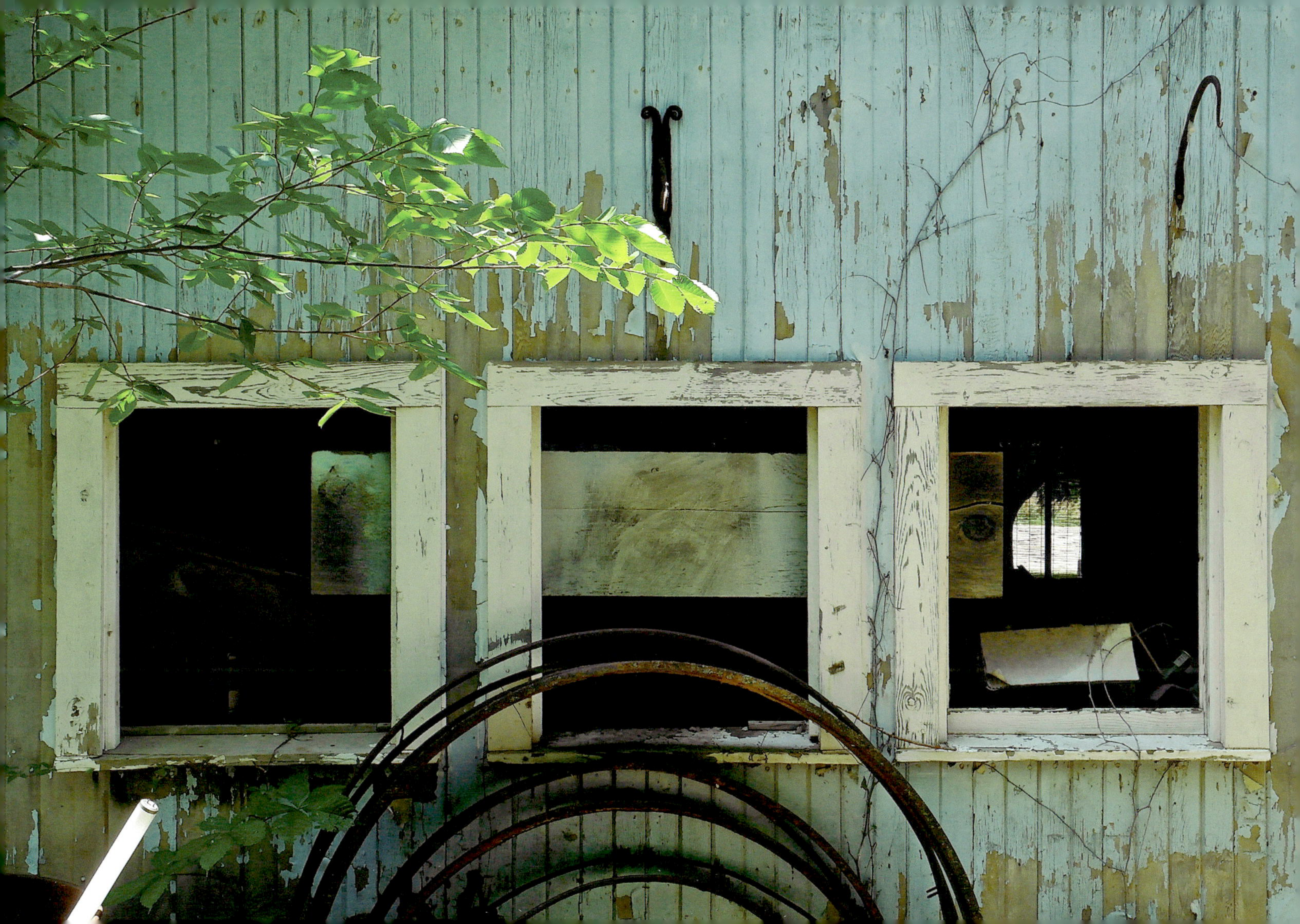

Ponder Paradox

How is the sky limited?
How is the sky unlimited?

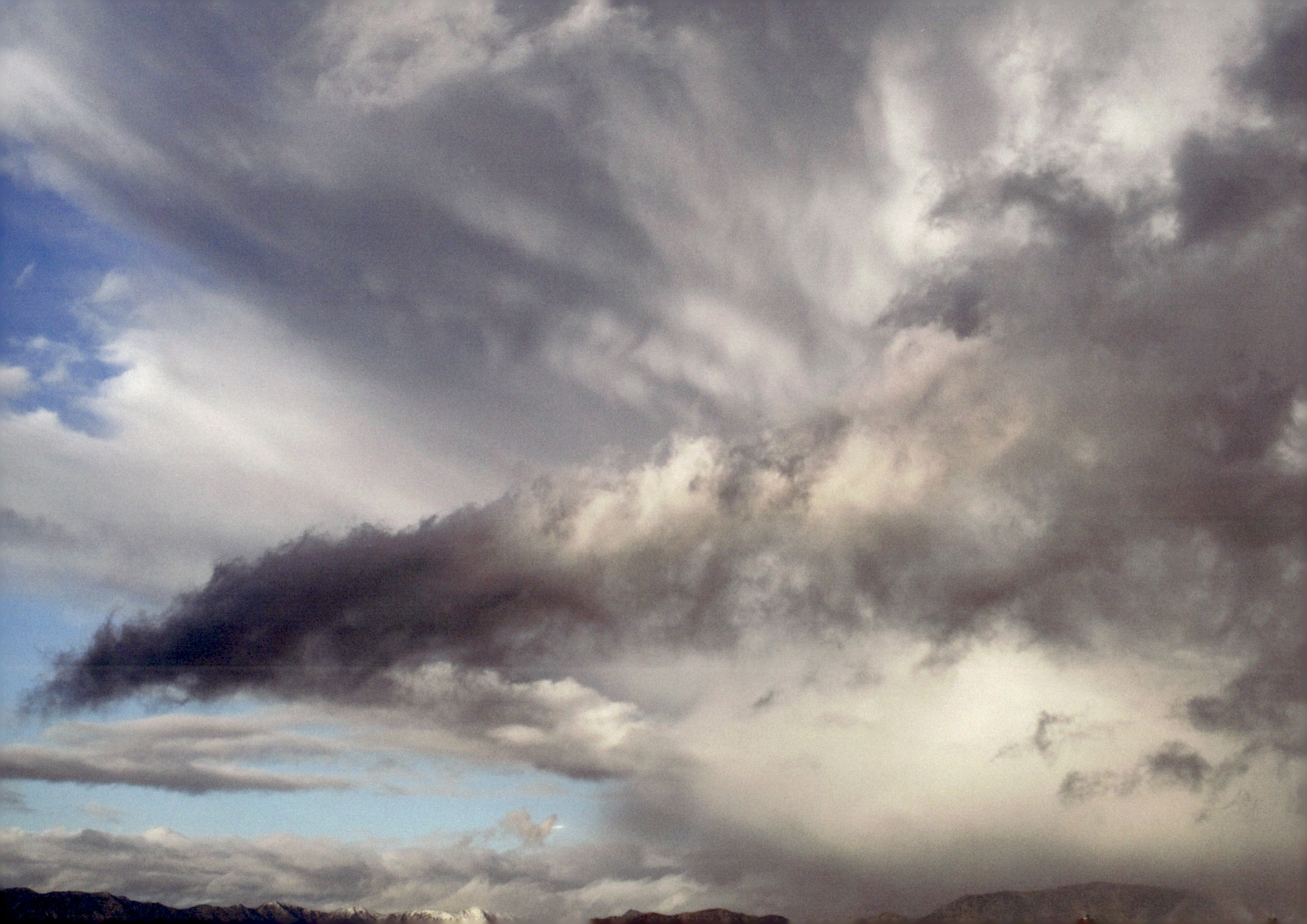

Sun Sinking

Squinting my eyes
The silent sun sinking in the west
Streams one billion rainbows

Wishing to the Light
To take me too
The beauty of the evening
Brings me back

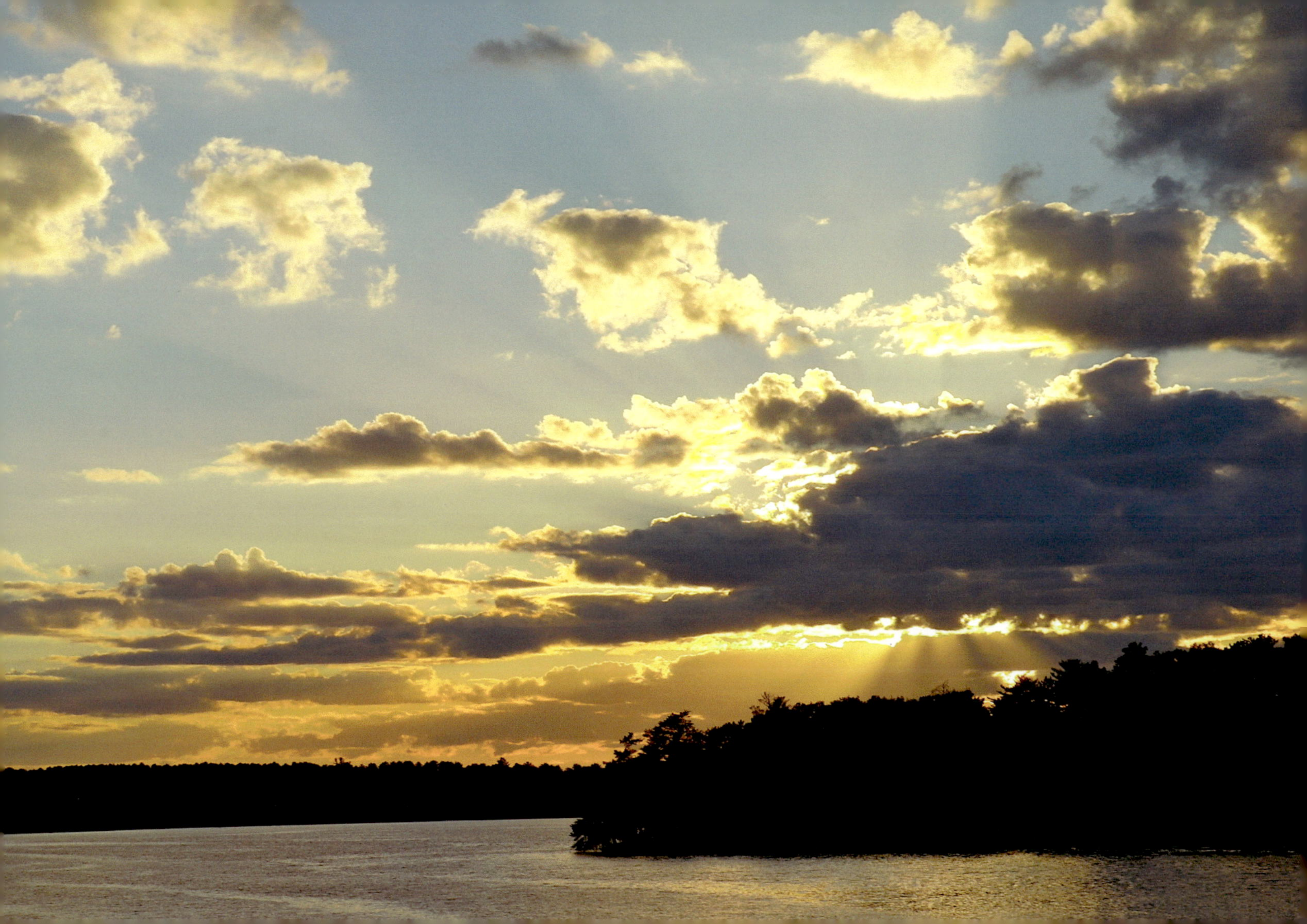

The Unknown You

You are layered deeper
Than you've ever been

Even with so many parts of you
Deep in the unknown
The unknown you is only one step away

One thin veil between
Your known and your unknown

Simply considering your very next step
Steps the unknown you
From one side to the other

Throw Sin Away

My sin sits there and stares at me
So I am going to throw my sin away
I begin to forgive myself
And soon my sin disappears

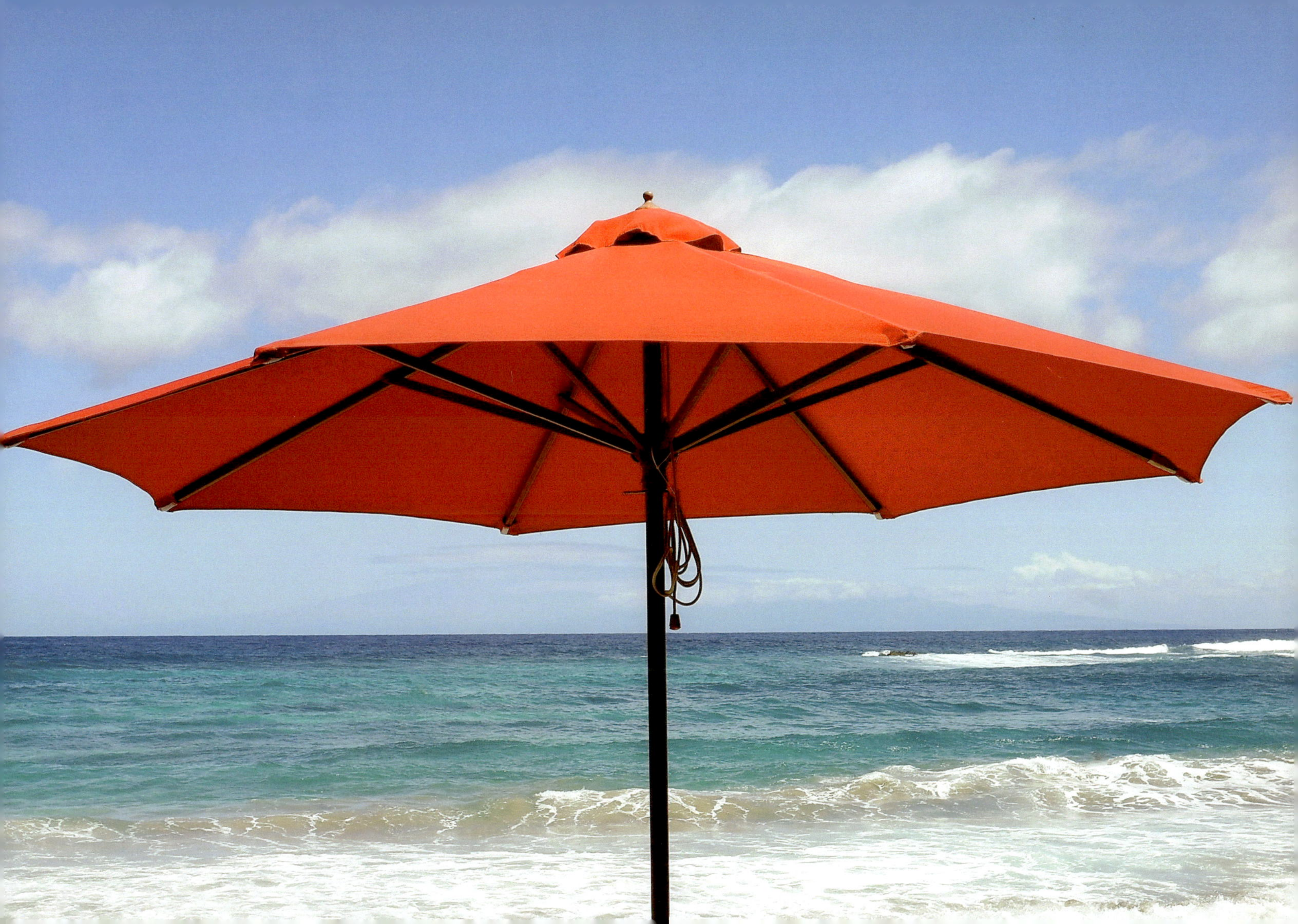

Together Magic

Red rosebud appears
White plum blossoms
Frame the scene
Together magic

My True Self appears
My Higher Self
Frames the scene
Together magic

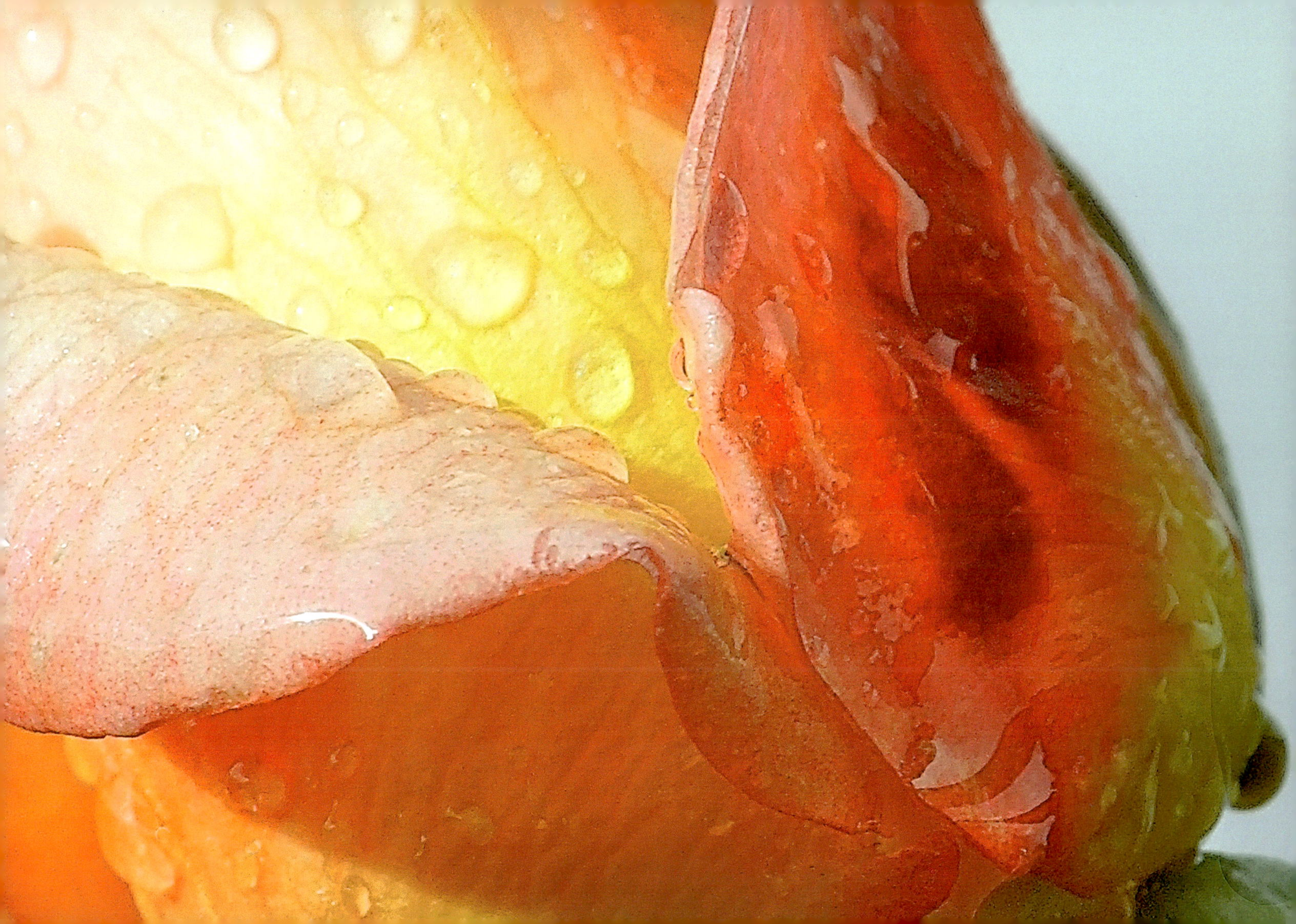

The Horse, the Cat, the Cow

Insignificance is rather arrogant
In the face of all that is
You are the exception
In all of creation
Complex to the max but insignificant?

Insignificance is a mask
To hold onto some dampening choice
To hide behind the weight
Of the mystery
Of whether to be significant or not

Whether to be significant or not
Is a calling that overspends on energy
Easier to surrender
That you already are significant
The horse, the cat, the cow

You Can Go On

Which will you embrace?
Birds singing
Or the past moaning?
Possibility or defeat?
Creating reality or reacting to reality?
New you or old you?

Birds singing so clear and true
So constant
What better metaphor do you need
Constant sound and song
Consistency in Nature
Showing the constancy of the ongoing

You do not stop
You are as constant as a bird's song
Embrace the future and you will find
The place to hear their song

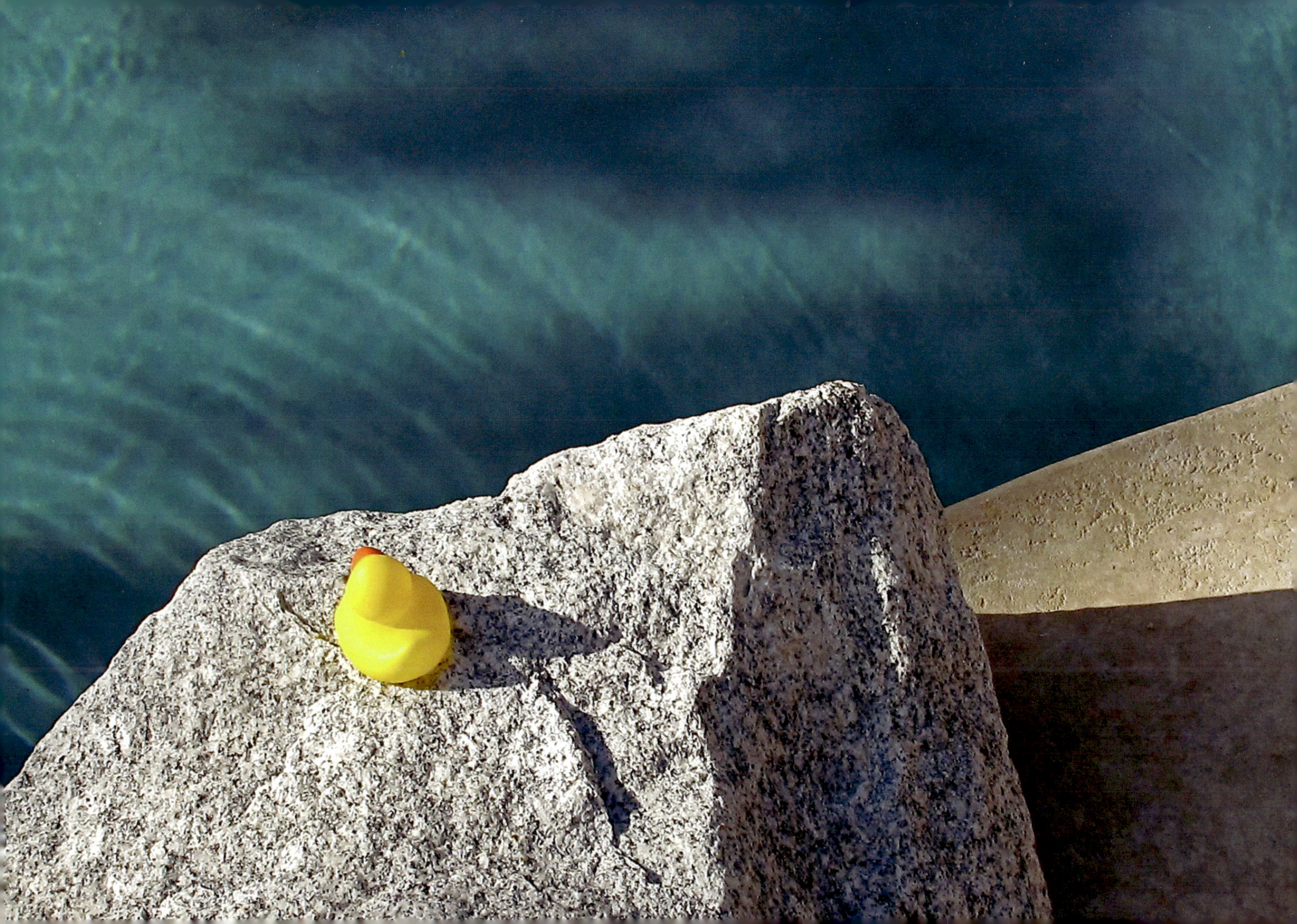

Unwrap Yourself

As you yearn
So you must follow
Unwrapping your gifts
Beats even the distractions
Of tears and of fears
Unwrap your gifts from the inside out
Unwrap what you seek
Unwrap yourself

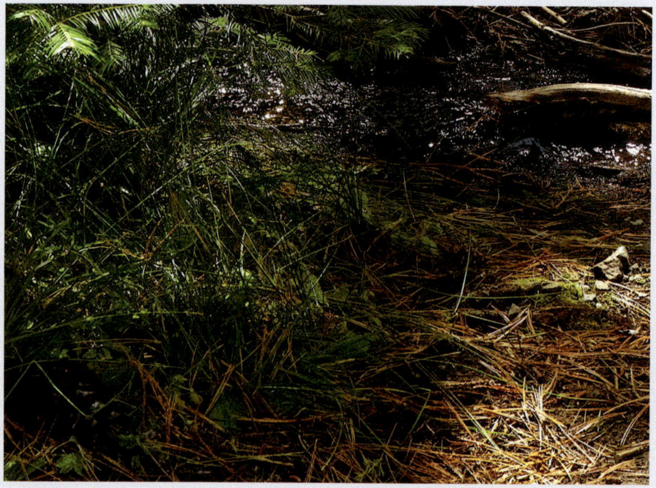

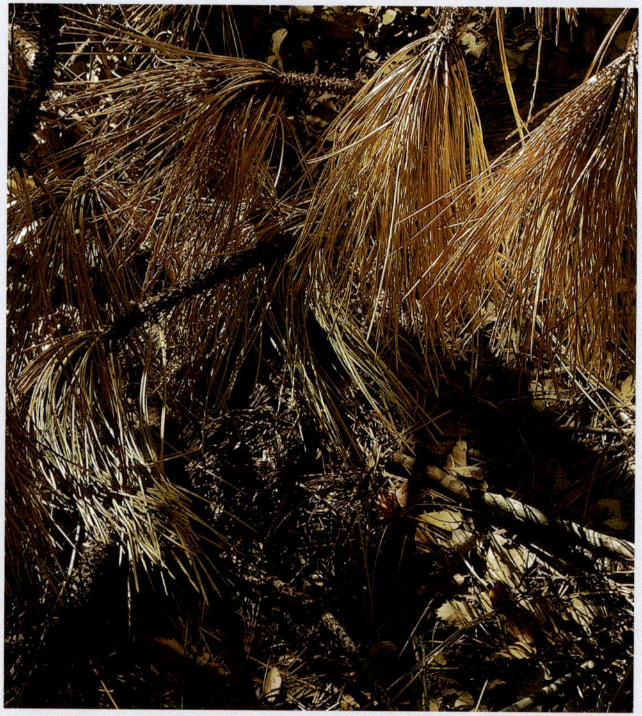

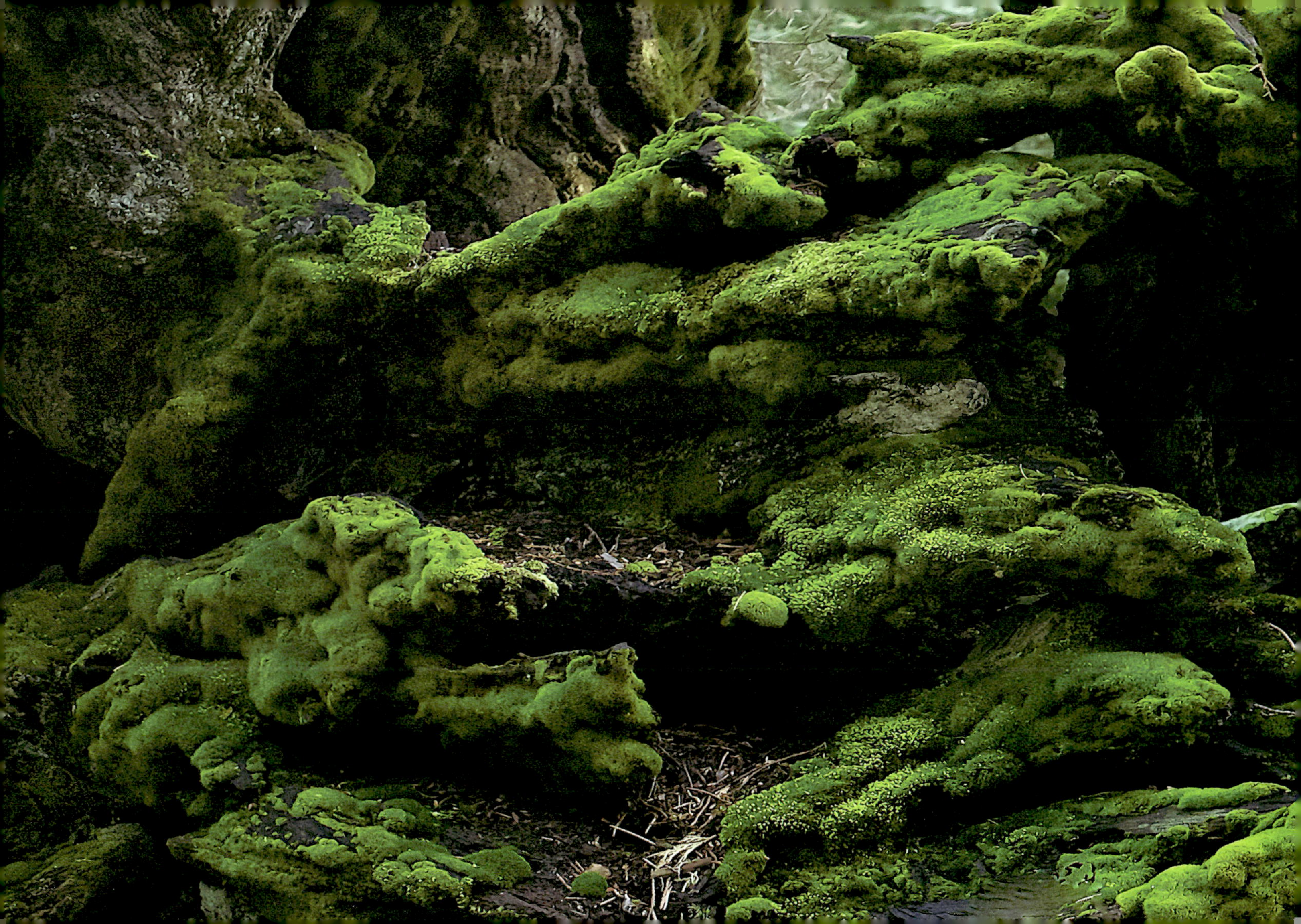

Wellness

Imagine into wellness
Come up with every pain and excuse
Follow every vibration
From every lifetime
Then feel it well

Feel into wellness
Clear every layer and every hurt
Of all resistance to change
Then feel it well

Soar to wellness
Float to wellness
Celebrate wellness
You can get well

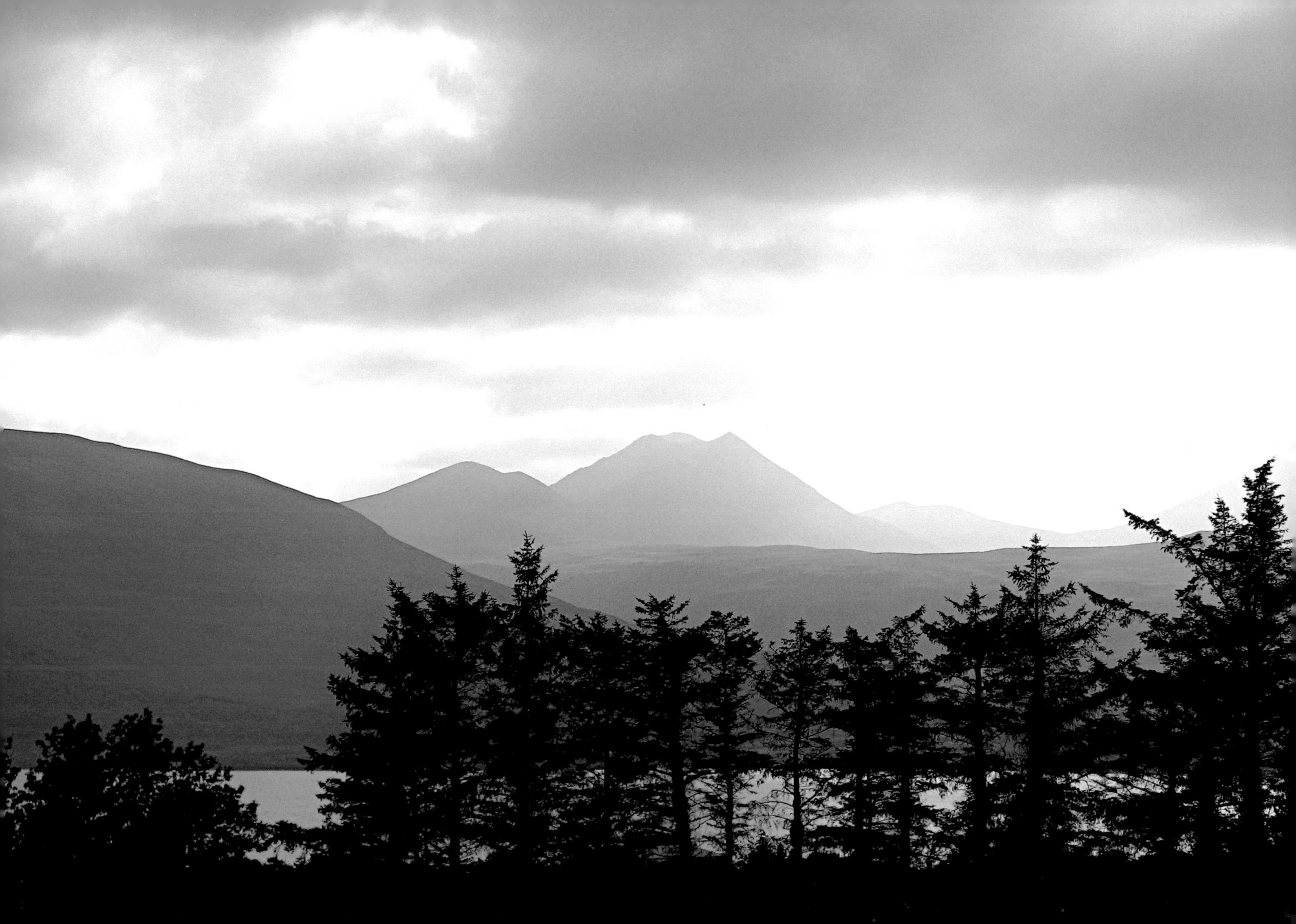

Make Time Last

Is there any way
To make time last?

Stay in between
The known and the unknown

Stay in the hush

Day after day
Night after night

No fears of exclusion
No fears of entropy
No fears of expansion

Long live the future

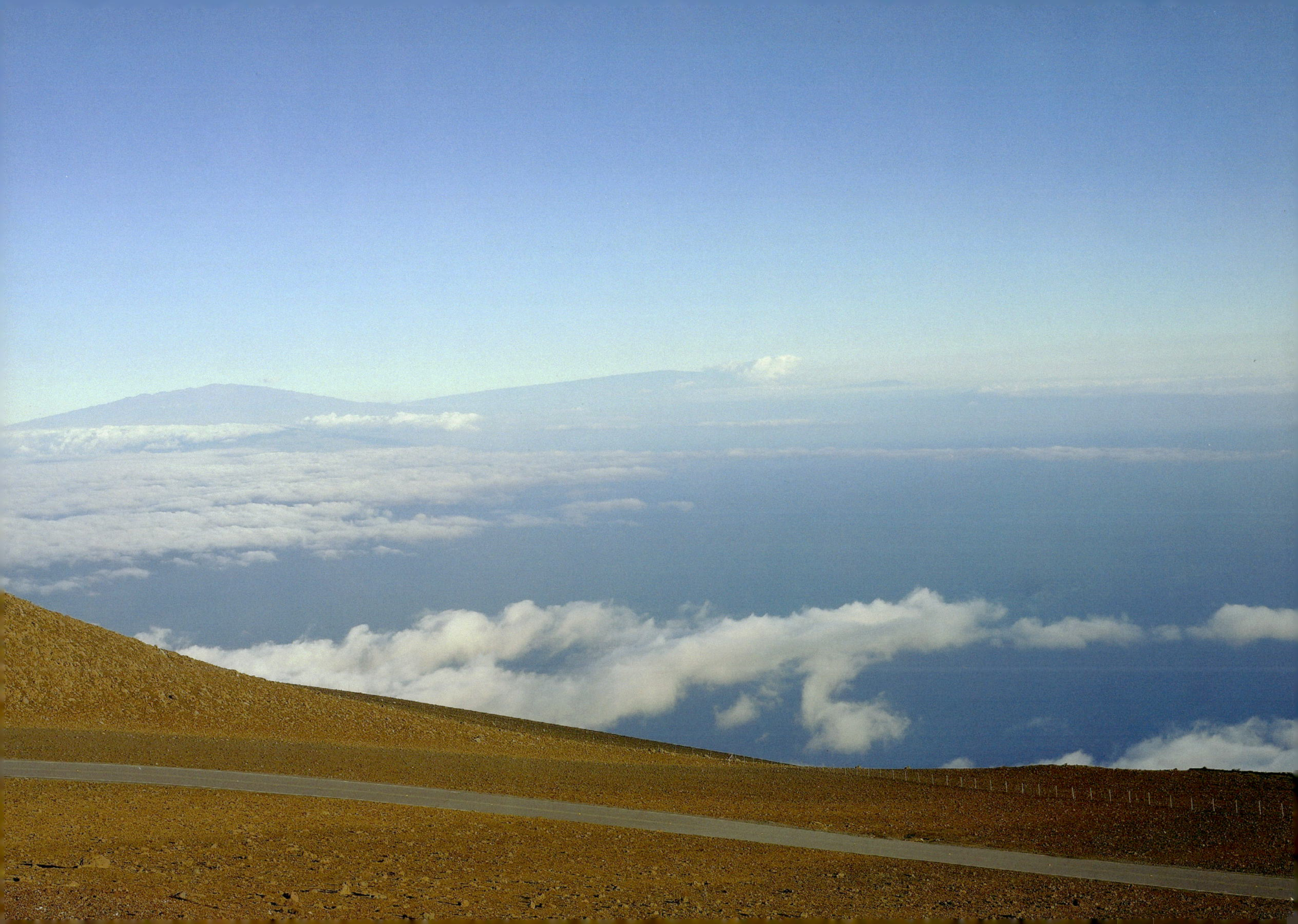

What Is Rest?

In all ways the unmanifest manifests

In resting and not resting
In doing and non-doing
In being and non-being

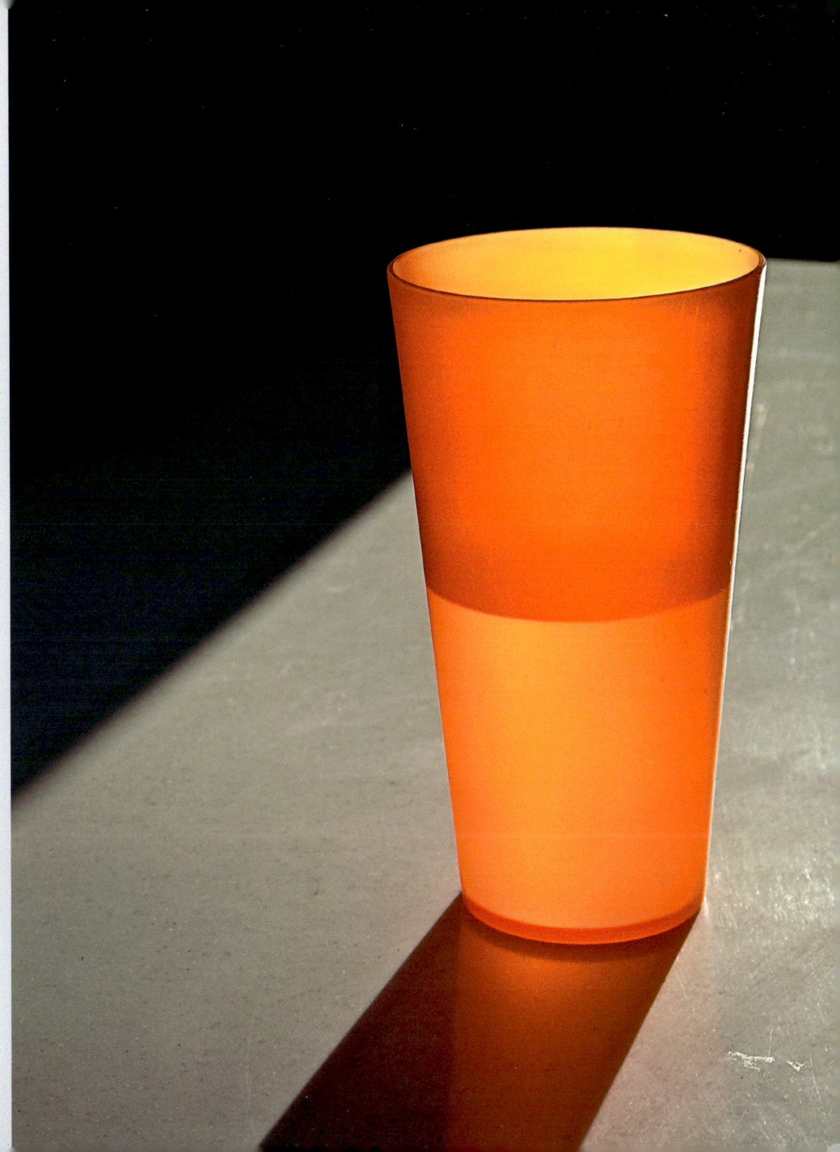

Very Special Thanks:

To my first listeners, my husband Bill and dear Celine;

To two who know all things design, print and kindness, Rachel and Greg;

To Howie Sann, my editor, for his great attention to detail and symmetry.

For a list of photo locations visit:

MaggieLynchPhotography.com